Community
Organization:
Conflict and
Reconciliation

# Community
# Organization:
# Conflict and
# Reconciliation

1344

Lyle E. Schaller

Nashville · Abingdon Press · New York

To George and Helen Brown

# Preface

During the 1950's thousands of local churches in American Protestantism began to take a renewed interest in their communities. There were several dimensions to this interest. In some neighborhoods this meant facing up to the question of racial discrimination. In several communities this interest was expressed in a new evangelistic thrust. In others the local church accepted responsibility for a specialized ministry to a specific group of persons such as homeless men, the residents of a public housing project, or persons receiving public assistance.

One of the first lessons that was learned from this new emphasis on "serving the people of our neighborhood" was that it was easier to offer the challenge than it was to develop an effective response. How do you help those who suffer from the handicaps of a dark skin, an inadequate education, or the emotional problems that grow out of a life in a broken home?

In a few cities leaders in the local churches decided that one of the church's primary responsibilities was to help the people organize to help themselves. It was believed that if the people in the neighborhood organized and assumed their place in the decision-making process they would be able to identify and solve many of their problems by themselves. By 1961 Chicago had become the most widely publicized example of how the local church might be involved in the community organization process. During the next four years churchmen all across America became interested in community organization as a tool of mission.

With this increase in interest came a growing division among churchmen over methods and techniques. One large and articulate group was primarily concerned with the pursuit of social justice. Another highly articulate group, perhaps smaller in size but equally determined, was primarily concerned with the legitimacy and propriety of the methods and techniques used in community organization.

By mid-1965 this surge of interest in community organization and the controversy over methods had spread to Buffalo, Cleveland, Detroit, Jersey City, Kansas City, Los Angeles, Rochester, San Francisco, Syracuse, and many other cities.

The purpose of this book is not to present a comprehensive statement on how a community may be organized. Nor is the purpose to offer a "how-to-do it" short course in community organization. Experts in the field, notably Murray Ross, have filled this need.

The goal has been to present a short, simple, and readable introduction to community organization which will help the typical churchman understand both the subject and the issues of this debate. The central purpose of this book is to help the reader ask himself the right questions when he encounters this process labeled "community organization."

While it will be obvious to the reader that I hold some rather strong opinions on various facets of the subject, a sincere effort has been made to be fair to both the proponents and the opponents of the use of conflict; to those who insist that the community organization process is the best way to solve the problems of poverty, racial discrimination, and blight, and also to those who argue that too often community organization is a disruptive force which impedes the efforts of the existing institutional structures.

The hope, of course, is that each side in this controversy will find in this volume a fair analysis of their position. The probability is that each side will conclude that the author has "sold out" to the opposing camp.

The reader should recognize that the church and American churchmen have long been involved in a great variety of efforts at community organization. One of the most common is the effort by social welfare workers to coordinate the work of the various agencies which are serving an overlapping clientele. Another is the neighborhood council which is formed to "stabilize" an all-white community when it appears that Negroes may move in. This book, however, is concerned with another type of community organization effort. This is the effort aimed at effecting social change rather than preserving the status quo. This is the effort to get at the root causes of the despair which result from a failure by the established structures of society, such as the churches and political parties, to meet their responsibilities. This is the effort to organize the deprived, the depressed, the dependent, and the disfranchised so they may be effective participants in the community decision-making process which so often affects but does not involve them. In this effort some churches and many churchmen are becoming involved in what may become the crucial power struggle in contemporary America. It is my opinion that no one should become a participant in the struggle without realizing the full implications of the struggle and of his involvement.

The first chapter offers an introduction to the subject and an explanation of how and why churches have become involved in community organization. This is followed by a discussion of planned social change, a concept which is essential to an understanding of the evolution of community organization from a field to a process. This evolution, including a discussion of the different types of community organization and the contributions of other disciplines, vocations, and organizations constitutes chapter three. These three chapters serve as an introduction to the current debate over the Christian's role in community organization.

One of the crucial elements in this debate centers on the use of conflict as a method of reaching the desired goals, and this issue is discussed in the fourth chapter. The conflict over the use of conflict first reached the level of a major controversy in church circles in Chicago where the methodology of Saul Alinsky has been accepted by scores of churchmen. This experience is summarized in chapter five. One of Alinsky's basic arguments is that the lot of the depressed and deprived cannot be improved until they acquire power, a point which troubles many churchmen who believe the primary goal of the Christian is reconciliation. An effort is made to present both sides of the debate in chapters six and seven. Chapter eight is a summary of the argument offered by those who oppose the growing interest of churchmen in community organization as a device for achieving social change. The last two chapters review some of the lessons which have been learned from experience by churchmen and suggest questions which merit serious study by anyone attempting an active role in this process of effecting social change.

In writing this book I have become heavily indebted to literally scores of people for their insights, ideas, and advice. The contributions of some are noted in the text or the footnotes. Several persons expressed a preference for anonymity and many are receiving it unjustly. Others who have made an especially significant contribution include David Barry, Arthur M. Brazier, Frank Countryman, James Davis, Philip Edwards, Ben Fraticelli, George A. Haddad, Huber Klemme, Alfred S. Kramer, Charles T. Leber, Jr., Reuben Lundeen, Robert H. MacRae, William E. Maloney, Richard E. Moore, Sheldon Rahn, David Ramage, Charles Rawlings, Seymour Slavin, John B. Turner, A. J. White III, Robert L. Wilson, and Frank Zeidler.

While these people contributed much to the content, obviously none of them can be held responsible for the errors of fact or interpretation which may be present in the book. Unfortunately, the responsibility for such errors must be borne by the author alone.

I am also grateful to the members of the governing Board of the Regional Church Planning Office who have provided me with the opportunity to observe the many facets of the Christian church in America.

LYLE E. SCHALLER

June 26, 1965

# Contents

Chapter One

# Who Really Cares?

"Before we turn to the agenda, is there anyone in the audience who would like to address this body?" With these words the president of the council opened a regular meeting of the city council in a small western city. It was the practice to hear visitors before proceeding with the routine business of the evening.

After a pause when it appeared that no one would respond, a middle-aged Negro farm worker in a blue work shirt and overalls rose. "Sir," he began, "could I have a few minutes of time to ask a favor of the city?"

"Certainly," responded the council president.

"Well, sir, there are a bunch of us colored families who live just outside the city limits, and our wells have all gone bad," began the Negro visitor. "Sir, I was wondering if it would be possible for the city to sell us some water. As it is now we have to haul our water more than a mile. We'd be willing to do anything you say, sir, if we could just get a little water for drinking and household use."

As the story unfolded it turned out the Negro visitor was the

15

spokesman for several Negro families who lived in a severely blighted ghetto just outside the central city. He had finally developed enough courage to come in and ask the city council for a little help with one of the community's biggest problems. Their wells yielded only water which was highly alkaline, and they were in desperate need of a reliable source of drinking water.

Shortly thereafter an agreement was reached whereby the city agreed to install a public water faucet with one meter. The Negro leadership had raised three hundred dollars as an advance deposit to guarantee that the city would be paid for installation of the water tap.

This experience reinforced the belief of many of the residents of the Negro ghetto. They knew the only way to deal with the white power structure was to beg for small favors with a great show of politeness and to settle for whatever the white leaders were willing to offer.

Six years later the same Negro who earlier had come begging with his hat in hand walked into city hall again. This time he was accompanied by four other men who served with him on the board of a newly formed utility district. This time he came not representing himself and a few other families, but rather representing an organized community of eighteen hundred residents, many of whom were Caucasians. This time he came armed with complete legal, engineering, and financial plans showing how and why the central city could and should cooperate in the installation of a public water supply system which would serve every home in his neighborhood. This time he was as polite as before, but this time he was treated with equal politeness. This time he was not ready to accept gratefully whatever proposal the city officials cared to offer. This time he came and sat with dignity as an equal at the bargaining table.

What had happened during these six years? What had changed this Negro leader's approach? What made the difference?

Two factors made the difference. Together they illustrate one of the most significant new developments in the life and ministry of the church in contemporary America.

First, although none of the residents of this Negro ghetto realized it, some people outside the ghetto cared. They were concerned about the people who lived in this suburban slum. As evidence of their concern they provided the necessary financial support for the appointment of a young community development specialist to serve this area.

Second, the man who was sent not only cared about people, he *possessed the training and skill to help the people help themselves.* Through a process known as *community organization,* he and his fellow workers helped the residents transform their neighborhood, their attitude toward the world, and, perhaps most important of all, their belief in themselves.

## What Is Community Organization?

Community organization is a relatively new concept. While community organization has been practiced by social workers and others for more than eighty years, for several decades it remained a very vague and elusive concept and lacked both definition and widespread acceptance. The first significant scholarly analysis of the subject was published as recently as 1955.[1]

[1] Murray G. Ross, *Community Organization—Theory and Principles* (New York: Harper & Row, 1955). The first textbook on community organization was by Jesse F. Steiner, *Community Organization: A Study of Its Theory and Current Practice* (New York: The Century Company, 1925). However it has little relevance to today's concepts of community organization.

Only during the last few years have leaders in the church come to recognize and accept community organization as a powerful tool that could be helpful to the parish pastor. The best known experience of the Protestant churches' involvement in community organization traces its beginnings back only to February, 1959.[2]

Community organization is a descriptive term which has been applied to a wide variety of activities and programs. More recently the definition of the phrase has been narrowed down to focus on a method or process of effecting social change.[3] In this process the residents of a community are organized so they are able to identify their problems, establish priorities among their needs, develop a program of action and move on to implement this program.

This problem-solving process emphasizes several considerations, including the recruitment and training of indigenous leaders, the right of local self-determination in the formulation of goals, the mobilization of local resources, and the use of democratic procedures; it usually is motivated in large part by discontent.

Normally the community referred to in the phrase "community organization" is a geographical area, and most efforts at organization have been based on the assumption that a community of interest will coincide with a geographical community. Thus community organization techniques are used in getting residents to band together to oppose an urban renewal project or to support a community improvement program or to win a referendum on a school bond issue.

[2] This reference is to The Woodlawn Organization (TWO) which has become the most widely publicized effort involving Protestant churches in the history of community organization. A description of TWO can be found in Chap. 5.

[3] For a variety of definitions of community organization, most of them developed by social workers, see Ernest B. Harper and Arthur Dunham, eds., *Community Organization in Action* (New York: Association Press, 1959), pp. 54-59.

As practiced today, however, community organization often resembles a social movement more than it does the earlier efforts at organization which were directed solely at the residents of a specific neighborhood or area. Today the community organization process closely parallels the definition of a social movement. It often is "a group venture extending beyond a local community or a single event and involving a systematic effort to inaugurate changes in thought, behavior and social relationships." [4]

Two of the most spectacular efforts at "community" organization in American history have been waged on a nongeographical base. The first of these was the organization of the employees of the automobile manufacturing plants carried on by the United Automobile Workers in the 1930's in which the community of interest was economic and vocational rather than geographical. The second is the Negro revolution which began in the mid 1950's and is based on a community of interest centering on ethnic, racial, and ideological considerations.

In both of these experiences most of the classic elements of the community organization process, and of a social movement, have been present. Both experiences vividly demonstrate how discontent and conflict may be crucial elements in effecting social change. Both also illustrate the problems of reconciliation which arise during rapid change. The use of conflict in achieving change often increases the degree of alienation and thus accentuates the need for reconciliation.

## Why the Sudden Interest in Community Organization?

As mentioned earlier, this sudden surge of interest in community organization goes back only a few years, although the practice

[4] This definition of a social movement is from C. Wendell King, *Social Movements in the United States* (New York: Random House, 1956), p. 27.

goes back several decades. The reasons for this recent growth of interest in community organization are many and varied. They include the continued urbanization of the population, the growth of public welfare agencies, the new interest in poverty, the unexpected problems which have accompanied urban renewal, the mechanization of agriculture and mining, the civil rights struggle, and the increase in leisure.

The most important single factor, however, has been the activity of the federal government. Here again, as in so many aspects of life, the decisions made in the nation's capital cause reactions in many vocations and professions all across the nation. While much of the impact on community organization has been indirect, in several areas there has been direct support for the basic concepts of self-determination, citizen participation, and planned social change. The direct interest of the federal government in community organization has been concentrated largely in what more accurately should be called community development.

For at least fifteen years the Department of Agriculture has encouraged the residents of rural communities to organize and come to grips with their problem through cooperative community action. This is a much more ambitious and sophisticated effort than the programs which were promoted by the county agricultural agent before World War II. Thirty years ago the organization of a soil conservation district was a major achievement. Today a rural community improvement association seeks to discover for itself what the needs are, rather than to go ask the county agent. The indigenous leadership, rather than the outside professional, analyzes local resources and decides on a course of action. It is this new leadership which clashes with the inherited power structure to revolutionize the local decision-making process.

The most spectacular effort by the federal government in accelerating the pace of social change has been the Peace Corps. Basically each Peace Corps member is a change agent hired by the United States to go and live in an overseas community and help the people organize to help themselves.

Not all the federal government's efforts to involve "the people" in the decision-making process at the local level have been overwhelmingly successful. One of the notable failures has been in urban renewal.

Indirectly, however, urban renewal has sparked community organization efforts in several large cities as the residents of areas to be renewed used the community organization process to gain a voice in the decision-making process. It is significant to note that this phase of community organization was not the result of a city-hall-directed effort, but rather came as a protest against the proposals which were offered by public officials. Thus in an indirect manner the federal urban renewal legislation has been responsible for some of the most notable examples of effective community organization that can be found anywhere in America.[5]

More recently the federal government has introduced two new major efforts at directly promoting community organization The first of these was the legislation creating the Area Redevelopment Administration (ARA). It was passed in 1961 to provide assistance to economically depressed areas. A central feature of this program was the creation of local community development organizations which would enable the residents of a depressed area to work out local solutions to local problems.

Of more far-reaching significance was Congressional approval

[5] For a more extensive evaluation of citizen participation and urban renewal see pp. 68-70.

of the Economic Opportunity Act (the "War on Poverty") in late 1964. The original legislation had two central themes, the retraining of unemployed persons and community action. Title II, which is the community action phase of the act, provides financial assistance from the federal government for local efforts at community organization. The goal is organization of the poor so they can articulate their needs, initiate action proposals, and gain a voice in the community decision-making process which will determine the weapons and strategy in the local campaign on the nationwide war against poverty.

Thus a concept which originated with a few social workers in Cincinnati in 1917 [6] and grew very slowly for four decades, has received its biggest single boost from the federal government.

This is not intended to be a criticism of the social work profession, but is offered only as an explanation for the sudden surge of interest in the subject of community organization.

While the social work profession has made the largest single contribution to the *art* of community organization, it ranks behind the federal government in its contribution to the *propagation* of the idea. This contribution has been limited for a variety of reasons. Among these has been the apparent unwillingness of most social workers to move against the community power centers or to make full use of the conflict theory in promoting social change. The emphasis which social workers have placed upon achieving social change through development of a consensus has been far less spectacular (but sometimes more effective) than efforts which have relied on the use of conflict. It has been

---

[6] For a detailed account of this pioneer effort in community organization see Wilbur C. Phillips, *Adventuring for Democracy* (New York: Social Unit Press, 1940).

the use of conflict, not reliance on development of a consensus, which has spurred recent interest in community organization.

The academicians in the field of social work, however, have systematized the basic concepts of community organization, trained field workers in the process, and brought the state of the art to its present level. Without the contributions of persons such as Jesse F. Steiner, Edward C. Lindeman, Clarence King, Leonard Mayo, Ernest B. Harper, Arthur Dunham, Murray G. Ross, and others the interested churchman would lack a systematically organized base of knowledge on which to build a program of church involvement in community organization.

The current interest in community organization cannot be explained adequately without reference to three other factors.

One is the use of many community organization techniques by the civil rights movement during the late 1950's and early 1960's. This has been especially significant because (a) many of the leaders in the movement have been prominent church leaders, (b) the civil rights movement has raised most clearly the question of the propriety of the use of conflict by Christians as they seek to effectuate social change, and (c) the civil rights struggle has also provided a prominent testing ground for the conflict theory of social change.

The second factor which has served to focus the attention of a comparatively large number of people on community organization has been the work of Saul Alinsky. The activities of this man who has become the most controversial figure in the field of community organization will be discussed in more detail in Chap. 5. It must be noted here, however, that his widely publicized efforts, especially in Chicago, have aroused widespread interest in the subject. In part this has been because Alinsky is a very effective promoter in securing financial support for his approach to community organization. In part it is because he has involved many churches, both Roman Catholic and Protestant, in community organization. These churches have become involved through their representatives (pastor and members) and also institutionally. Finally it must be recognized that in part Alinsky's impact has been a result of his dramatic personality.

The third factor has been a growing dissatisfaction in America, especially in the large urban centers, with the existing structures of society, both political and social. The criticism is made that the needs of the people, especially those on the bottom rungs of the social and economic ladder, have been ignored for too long. Efforts to correct this situation have focused on the community organization process as a means of overcoming the apathy of the powerless and the self-centeredness of the powerful.

## The Church's Stake in Community Organization

"Should the church become involved in community organization?" "Is it right for the church to participate?" "Can a good Christian be active in this sort of thing?"

Questions such as these are being asked in many church circles today. They are difficult to answer because they are the wrong questions. The basic questions which churchmen should ask are not "If" questions, but are "How" questions.

Prior to the "How" question, however, is the "Why" question. Why is the church involved in community organization? There are two dimensions to the answer to this question—theological and institutional.

Theologically, the answer is simple and clear. Through the centuries the church has been the one social institution which has really cared for the poor, the oppressed, the downtrodden, and the deprived. This concern has reflected God's love for his children as expressed in the birth, life, death, and resurrection of Jesus Christ. The church of Jesus Christ has always cared. A part of this concern has been the individual Christian's love of his fellow man, and inextricably woven into this has been the love of justice. Collectively, Christians can express this love of man and concern for justice through their church.

Now a tool has been developed which helps the church to express this concern more effectively. The assumptions, goals, and process of community organization have begun to replace the nineteenth-century concept of charity with a response which appears to many to be more compatible with the New Testament definition of charity. Through the use of the community organization process people are able to grow, to gain a new dignity, and to become effective participants in the decision-making processes which affect their own lives. The community organization process is a method of human resource development—a means by which the church may help the individual come closer to fully developing the potential which the Creator has placed in each human being.

Add to this historic concern of the church for the dispossessed, the powerless, the persecuted, and the poor, the idea that this is to be a *neighbor-centered* concern, and one can begin to see the unique role of the church in community organization. There are many other forces in our society which are eager, willing, and able to organize people; however, all of these other organizing forces either initially or eventually begin to become *self*-centered. This is as true of labor unions as it is of political clubs, or civil rights organizations, or social welfare agencies. It is true because this is the corrupting nature of power in the hands of sinful men. This is also the biggest risk the church faces when it becomes involved in community organization, but the church has a divine imperative to be and to remain neighbor-centered in its mission. This should reduce (but not eliminate) the risk. It is also the basic theological reason why the church cannot ignore this new tool and remain a faithful servant.

A variety of other specific theological arguments could be offered to support the church's involvement in community organization—based on the relationship of the church and the world, the crucifixion, the doctrine of man, creation, sin, the incarnation, and other Christian doctrines. However, that is neither the theme of this book nor the special competence of the author. Suffice it to say that the church's concern for justice and its call to minister to persons as individual children of God justifies its involvement in this special area of activity.

Lest anyone conclude that the sole concern of the church in community organization is with the oppressed and the poor, and much of the most widely publicized efforts by the church would tempt one to come to this conclusion, it should be pointed out that the church also has a ministry to those who are attacked by newly created community organizations, to those who are labeled as the oppressors and exploiters. This too is a part of the church's call in community organization. Jesus told his followers, "Love your enemies, do good to those who hate you, bless those who curse you, pray for those who abuse you." (Luke 6:27-28.) One aspect of this ministry is discussed in Chap. 7.

Institutionally, the church also has good reason to be involved in community organization. Through the centuries the Christian church has operated primarily on the basis of the geographical parish. Despite the large number of congregations which have abandoned the concept of the geographical parish, *they have been exceptions to both the dominant tradition of the church and to the current assumptions which guide most of the decision*

*makers of most local churches and most denominational agencies.*
Today the assumption that the local church exists to serve the
people who live in the community in which the church building
is located is widely accepted. (It is also true that this assumption
is articulated more often than it is followed—but that is another
problem.)

Therefore, if one accepts the principle that the local church
exists to serve its community, it is difficult to see how it can expect to do this without becoming involved, either directly or
indirectly through its members, in the dynamics of social change
in that community. As mentioned earlier, however, human resource development, not the effecting of social change, should be
the *primary* motive for the churches' involvement in community
organization. Frequently this does mean that the church must
become an influential factor in the process of social change and
the community organization process is an apppropriate means
of achieving social change.

Community organization offers the church and the churchman
the opportunity to be an active and constructive participant in
the community decision-making process. Thus the church is able
to contribute its insights and values to the change process, to
present and represent the Christian ethic in the debate of social
issues, and to become a partner in neighborhood efforts of service
and compassion.

From an institutional point of view, perhaps the most interest-
ing aspect of the churches' involvement in community organization is the role of the home missions officials and agencies of
Protestantism. Recently an informal alliance has been developed
between the social action wing of Protestantism, which always
has been interested in influencing the course of social change,
and the home missions departments. In several Protestant de-

nominations the staff members of the home missions department have expressed a much greater interest in community organization than have the staff members of the social action agencies. This can be seen most clearly in The United Presbyterian Church in the U.S.A., but it is also true in the United Church of Christ, The Protestant Episcopal Church, and, to a lesser extent, in The Methodist Church and the Christian Church.

This reflects the insight of a churchman who is also a well-known figure in community organization and who has written, "Efforts to secure social changes which increase the level of justice are important to mission." [7] As the church seeks to fulfill its mission in a complex society, it finds itself forced to accept new responsibilities and to influence social change. Community organization has emerged as a process which is relevant to this new sense of mission.

In reviewing the reasons for this wave of interest in community organization as a tool of mission, a word of warning is also in order. There is the ever present danger that this may develop to the proportions of a fad and pervert the mission and purpose of the church. One of the seldom mentioned reasons for some churchmen's interest in community organization is a sense of guilt over the past aloofness and inactivity of the churches. This feeling of guilt has been intensified by the civil rights movement and similar areas of political action. Thus there is the threat that the community organization process may be accepted as *the* mission of the church rather than as a tool which can be helpful in fulfilling the mission. This threat becomes more serious when the churches' participation in community organization is uncritically accepted and promoted.

[7] Douglas Still, "The Churches and Community Organization," a mimeographed paper published by the Department of Social Welfare of the Church Federation of Greater Chicago. Undated, p. 2.

Today's churchman who seeks to become an active, but critical, participant in this new dimension of mission may find it helpful to review the emergence of this process known as community organization. Before doing that, however, it is necessary to examine the relationship of the church to planned social change.

Chapter Two

# The Church and Social Change

As they left the garden, Adam is alleged to have said, "Eve, we are living in an era of transition."

From the beginning of time man has been confronted with the fact of change—and has responded by refusing to believe it. Almost any kind of social change inevitably produces problems. For most people and most social institutions any deviation from the accustomed pattern not only represents change, it also represents the threat of the unknown, the untested, and the unfamiliar. Churchmen may joke about living in an era of transition, but underneath the humor lies an uneasiness brought on by the knowledge that the changes which are a part of the transition produce new problems. Furthermore, any attempt to solve these problems probably will produce further changes which in turn create new problems.

Thus people who turn to the church from a world of change and uncertainty expect, or at least hope, to find reassuring stability and tranquillity. This, added to normal institutional pressures, often forces the church to take a conservative position which is contrary to the gospel preached from the pulpit. This conservatism in the church is manifested in a variety of ways. The church which is relocated from what was once a "good" neighborhood in the central city out to a new site in suburbia where the members (or at least the leaders) now live is an example of a social system moving to a new environment in the hope that the old methods and processes will function better in an environment which resembles the old, but now greatly changed, neighborhood. The decision to shift the major worship service of the week from 11 A.M. to 9:30 A.M. on Sunday is a conservative reaction to the revolution wrought by a shortened work week which sees many families out of the city from Friday afternoon until Sunday evening. The continuation of all-white congregations meeting in churches located in neighborhoods that have become predominantly Negro is a conservative reaction to social change. Each of these three changes calls for a more radical adjustment than the church is willing to make.

It is important to distinguish among (1) the natural institutional conservatism of the church as a social system, (2) the role of the church as a conserver and transmitter of desirable religious and social values, and (3) the response of the individual Christian to social change. The individual churchman may feel constrained by the imperative of the gospel to favor a much more radical course of action than his church is able to adopt. This is normal. The individual or small group almost always has a greater variety of alternatives open than does a much more complex social system which is more dependent on a consensus and which has a vested interest in preserving the status quo. This difference is one of the greatest sources of tension as Christians and churches are confronted with the challenge to participate in the community organization process.

Despite its conservative nature, however, the church is a dynamic social system. It is changing. Most of the changes are slow and come through adaptation, adjustment, and reorganization, but change is occurring. Often the church reacts to changes in other social systems, seldom does the church initiate changes which influence or greatly alter the other structures and systems of society. The church tends to be a reactor to change rather than a creator of change. There are exceptions to this generalization, and these usually develop when some of the leaders of the church see the existing social structure as imperfectly embodying the values which the church seeks to conserve and transmit. The role of the Protestant churches in the prohibition movement represented such an exception. To a limited extent the involvement of the church in the civil rights movement is another, although here the church was slow to assume a position of leadership, and many churches and churchmen have stayed out of the struggle and a few have even opposed it.

When one examines the role of the church either in America or in the world scene, it becomes very evident that there is little unanimity in the church today on the church's responsibilities in an era of rapid social change.[1]

In discussing the role of the church on the contemporary world scene one observer pointed out three dilemmas in which the church finds itself in a rapidly changing society. The local church in a changing community often finds itself in the same three dilemmas. The first of these is the realization that the goals of progress, social justice, and freedom often are incompatible, especially if pursued at the same point in history. Frequently a choice must be made from among the three. A second dilemma

[1] Paul Abrecht, *The Churches and Rapid Social Change* (New York: Doubleday and Co., 1961), p. 197.

arises from the fact that the tensions created by change often threaten the institution. Thus a local church may be so threatened and made so insecure by the changes occurring in the neighborhood that it is immobilized. Finally social change may force the local church into the dilemma of having to choose between "the inadequate past and the uncertain future." [2] This, too, may cause the church to be slow to respond to the changes going on all around it.

This analysis should help the community organizer to be more understanding when he finds a local church in which the leaders appear to be sympathetic toward the goals of his organization but the congregation never quite "gets around" to voting to participate. Normal, natural social pressures tend to make the local church assume a conservative position. At times this may be reflected by apparent indecision, at other times by open opposition to proponents of change.

## Planned Social Change

This normal adverse reaction by the church, and by many churchmen, to individuals and organizations which propose change may be reduced if the idea of change is presented in terms of alternatives. Social change is occurring continuously, often without direction or plan. Is it preferable for the community and the church to simply respond, sometimes through adaptation, sometimes by inaction to these changes? Or would it be better for the community to take the initiative and plan for social change? While a third alternative of simply maintaining the status quo may be thought to be the most attractive, this choice does not exist in the world of reality. In a dynamic society change is al-

[2] *Ibid.*, pp. 198-99.

ways occurring for the word "dynamic" means change. Therefore, which is the more desirable, planned or unplanned change?

As individuals and as families, Americans accept the idea of planned change. The semi-annual trip to the dentist, the almost universal acceptance of social security, the savings account to help a child through college, and the family health insurance program are illustrations of how individuals accept the inevitability of change, plan at least to be prepared for it, and even to influence the change pattern.

When we move up to the more complex level of social systems which are called organizations one also sees an almost universal acceptance of planned change. Each year motor companies plan to place a new line of automobiles on the market. The local school plans to introduce new foreign language courses and to use a new method of teaching mathematics. The local church holds a series of special training classes for Sunday school teachers to help prepare them for the new curriculum which is to be published by the denomination next year. Each of these actions represents an acceptance of change and the preparation of a plan for responding to change.

At the community level of our hierarchy of social systems often there is a reluctance to plan for change. Of course, there are exceptions to this generalization. However almost invariably these exceptions are where a single community has a political identity as a village or city. Thus there may exist an excellent set of zoning ordinances and subdivision regulations which are used to guide changes in the land-use pattern. Or the municipality may have a Human Relations Committee to help direct the response to pressures for racial integration.

Most cities and many villages, however, are composed of a number of communities. Rarely are the people who reside in one of these communities organized to function as a separate social system. If the residents are not organized, it is impossible for that community to respond as a community. It cannot plan for social change. In unorganized communities the planning for social change can be carried on only at other levels of society. This may be the city government which plans for the city as a whole (a set of communities). Or the city may plan for change in each community; however, when this occurs it usually means the planning is being done *for* the community by outsiders and not *by* the people of the community.

In addition the various organizations in the community may have their own plans for dealing with social change, but obviously these are individual plans of separate organizations and in no way can these become an adequate substitute for a comprehensive plan in which the goals and procedures for attaining those goals are determined by the residents as an organized group. Furthermore, if two or more organizations in a community do have a plan, it is doubtful they are compatible, and even if they are, they represent the thinking only of those few organizations and not of all the residents of the community.[3]

The purpose of community organization is to fill this gap, to organize the residents of the community so they can take a positive role in planning for the inevitable changes which are certain to occur.[4]

[3] Most of the present emphasis on the word "community" in community organization and community planning can be traced back to the contributions of Robert E. Park and Ernest W. Burgess at the University of Chicago. A brief account of their contributions can be found in the first chapter of Ernest W. Burgess and Donald J. Bogue, eds., *Contributions to Urban Sociology* (Chicago: The University of Chicago Press, 1963) pp. 1-14.

[4] A series of good brief essays on planned social change can be found in Robert Morris, ed., *Centrally Planned Change: Prospects and Concepts* (New York: National Association of Social Workers, 1964). The lead article by James Q. Wilson, "An Overview of Theories of Planned Change," is especially helpful. Another useful, but much more general, collection of articles in Amitai Etzioni and Eva Etzioni, eds., *Social Change* (New York: Basic Books, 1964).

## Theories of Social Change

These changes occur as the result of social processes which are always at work in all social systems. Sociologists usually identify four or five separate processes—cooperation, competition, conflict, accommodation, and assimilation.[5] Some sociologists, however, suggest a twofold definition which is very useful in a study of community organization—cooperation and opposition.[6] This definition is based on the assumption that the persons and organizations involved in the social process are either working together or working in opposition. In either case change is the result.

The distinction between the definitions is not as great as may first appear. Accommodation and assimilation are really descriptions of social change, leaving three processes as causes of social change—cooperation, competition, and conflict. Furthermore, these are not as mutually exclusive as they may appear. Competition may become so acute that it turns into conflict, or it may fade away and be indistinguishable from cooperation. Furthermore, conflict does not exist apart from competition.

The relevance of this framework for analyzing social change can be illustrated by the reaction to an urban renewal proposal for the South End neighborhood in the mythical city of Glendale. Glendale is a typical midwestern city with a population of 50,000, a mixed economy, and an "across the tracks" neighborhood known as South End. As defined by the city planning commission, South End is a community with a population of 3,800, one fourth of whom are Negroes and Puerto Ricans. According to the 1960 census of housing 69 per cent of the housing units are in structures which are either dilapidated or deteriorating. The neighborhood

[5] Lowry Nelson, Charles E. Ramsey, and Coolie Verner, *Community Structure and Change* (New York: The Macmillan Company, 1960), p. 393.

[6] David O. Moberg, *The Church as a Social Institution* (Englewood Cliffs, N. J.: Prentice-Hall, 1962), p. 267.

is split between two different wards and neither of the councilmen live in South End. On one edge of the community is located the Methodist Hospital, and also bordering the South End community are the buildings of a State Teachers College which is expanding to become a liberal arts school which will offer some graduate training.

After the city has prepared a preliminary plan for the renewal of the area a series of informal informational meetings are held throughout the South End neighborhood. At each of these meetings the urban renewal officer for the city begins with a few introductory comments.

"This is not a formal public hearing, that will come later, rather this is an effort by the city to enlist the help of the residents and property owners of this neighborhood. We solicit your comments, your criticisms, your ideas, your suggestions. We want the final plan to reflect your wants and needs as much as possible.

"Some of you already have asked why we have prepared this plan before coming out here to hear your suggestions. Let me emphasize as strongly as I can that this is only a preliminary proposal. It is not final. We prepared it for two reasons. First, to provide a point of departure for our discussions with you. Second, because there are certain technical aspects of the proposal which can be prepared only by trained specialists—these include the design of the major traffic arteries, the location of utility lines and similar technical matters. However, this is only a proposal, not a final plan. Nothing about it is sacred; it can be changed."

It was clear to all that implementation of the renewal proposal would produce tremendous social changes in South End. How would the community react to planned social change? Three possible reactions illustrate how an understanding of social processes provides a framework for understanding community organization.

One possible reaction to the city's plan would be for representatives from business groups, the schools, the hospital, the college, and a few other organizations to get together to discuss the proposal. Most of these people were not surprised by the city's tentative plan, for they had been contacted by city officials during the earliest stages of the preparation of the preliminary plan. While each one probably has a few reservations about the plan, and perhaps even some suggestions for improvements, these people are in general agreement that the area needs renewal treatment. Therefore, they decide to *cooperate* with the city, to help promote support for the idea, to raise money to influence a favorable vote on the referendum which will be necessary for financing the city's share of the cost, and to form a committee which will attempt "to reason" with any opponents who may appear. In return for their cooperation they expect the city officials to be willing to make several changes in the plan. These changes will eliminate most of the reservations held by the members of the group.

In return for this support the city government will be able to demonstrate to the Housing and Home Finance Agency that it has had "citizen participation" in the preparation of this proposal. From the community organization perspective this is an example of planned social change accomplished through the process of *cooperation or collaboration*.

A second type of community response to the city's renewal proposal would be for about the same group of community leaders to get together when they first heard the city was considering the renewal of South End. Because of previous differences with the present city administration they were apprehensive. They suspected that the interests they represented would not receive proper consideration.

After a couple of meetings they decided to establish a non-profit development corporation which would be financed through contributions from the businesses and institutions which might be affected by a renewal program. This development corporation then proceeded to hire a planning consultant who prepared a renewal plan which (a) was in harmony with federal requirements for matching funds, and (b) took into consideration the vested interests of all firms, institutions, and persons who had contributed to the establishment of the development corporation.

A week before the city officials were planning to release their proposal to the press, the local newspaper carried a front page story of the plan developed by the South End Development Corporation "which represented the desires of the people who live, work, and own property in the area."

In this case the *threat* of planned social change touched off a process of *competition*. In effect these leaders had established a pseudogovernmental planning agency to compete with the city's planning operation. The two would be in competition for the necessary public approval, and this competition would be the process which would determine the nature of the changes in South End. At this stage this was clearly a process of competition. Subsequent events could alter this. The community leaders might be able to develop an acceptable compromise plan with the city and thus move to a process of *cooperation or collaboration*. On the other hand it might be impossible to work out a satisfactory compromise. The city officials would insist on their plan and the community leaders would be adamant in their opposition to the city's proposal. In this event the process of social change would probably move from one of *competition* to *conflict*.

Another possible reaction to the city's proposal might occur as a result of the adverse reaction of many residents to the proposal. The preliminary plan called for the clearance of some eighty acres of land near the hospital and college. Part of this area was earmarked for sale to the two institutions to assist them in their expansion plans. The remainder was designated for medium high density residential use. When asked what this meant the city officials explained that market surveys had determined there was a demand for apartments in the area which would rent for about thirty to fifty dollars per month per room. They added that the expansion of the hospital and college would increase this demand and so they had allocated forty acres of land for residential use to be redeveloped at an average density of twenty-five units per acre.

The only two buildings to be left standing in the area were St. Mark's United Presbyterian Church and St. Joseph's Roman Catholic Church. The reuse plan included the reservation of one acre of land for St. Mark's and three acres for St. Joseph's. The initial reaction of the leaders at the two churches was that the renewal plan might be a blessing. It would provide badly needed offstreet parking for the Presbyterian Church and an opportunity to enlarge the tiny playground at the Catholic Church. Both churches would be able to buy this land at "marked down" prices because of the federal subsidy for the clearance program.

On second thought, however, serious questions began to be voiced. What provision was being made to rehouse the 2,600 persons who would be displaced by the clearance program? Would this plan drastically alter the ministry and outreach of the two churches? Would this destroy South End as a community? Why was it necessary to raze all buildings? One third were in sound condition, and many others could be rehabilitated. If these were not demolished, the relocation problem would be cut in two. Many of those who were to be displaced were Negroes; would they be able to find another place to live? Most of those to be displaced, both white and Negro, would have great difficulty in finding replacement housing at rents even close to what they now were paying.

After months of raising these questions and failing to get what they deemed to be satisfactory answers, the pastors of the two churches had developed a very close relationship. Both of them had been besieged by complaints and questions from their parishioners, most of whom were bewildered, awed, frightened, or overwhelmed by the renewal plan. When their protests had failed to receive more than a polite brush-off, the two clergymen decided they would have to fight power with power. They set out to organize a community council, believing that a protest from an organized group of residents and organizations would carry more weight at city hall.

A year to the day after the mayor had announced the preliminary renewal plan for South End he arrived at city hall to find himself greeted by pickets carrying placards which bore slogans such as, "We Want a Democracy, Not a Dictatorship," "Urban Renewal Is Negro Removal," "Keep South End for the South Enders," and "Find Us a Home Before You Evict Us."

That same week the mayor discovered that the South End Citizens Council was attempting to halt the recertification of the city's workable program for urban renewal by protesting the lack of citizen participation. If successful this would mean the cutting off of federal matching funds for the South End renewal project.

In this case the prospect of planned social change found one group of persons finally resorting to *conflict* in their efforts to gain a voice in the planning for change.

The urban renewal episode in Glendale also could be used to illustrate a fourth social process—*accommodation*. In many cities similar projects have encountered little neighborhood opposition. The residents and businesses of the project area who are to be displaced accept the proposal and perhaps one half to two thirds

41

go out on their own and find new homes. The institutions feed the renewal proposal into their own internal planning and accommodate themselves to the changes which will result from implementation of the plan. All are reactors to externally planned change; none are initiators of change.

Perhaps the most familiar example of how one area of social change includes all five social processes is the change in relationship between Caucasians and Negroes in America. During the past three and one-half centuries this has moved from one of slave-master relationship *toward* one of equality.

This change has been resisted by many whites who were willing to use the process of *conflict* to slow or halt the change. This use of conflict included beatings, riots, and lynchings. At various points in this struggle a few Negroes were willing to use conflict to accelerate the rate of change. This has included such events as the insurrections led by Denmark Vesey and Nat Turner, a few riots in northern cities, and more recently a long series of events in which conflict was the tool of those seeking social change. Recent illustrations of the use of conflict include demonstrations in dozens of southern cities, the wade-ins in St. Augustine, the Philadelphia economic boycott, the Harlem riots, and the use of civil disobedience in Cleveland.

For most of the years since the first slaves were brought to Virginia by a Dutch ship in 1619, however, this relationship has been marked more by *accommodation and assimilation* than by conflict, competition, or cooperation. Most Negroes had to accommodate themselves to the changes which occurred as a result of the Civil War, the thirteenth amendment, the technological advances in agriculture which reduced the need for hand labor, and the urbanization of America. Negroes did not have a voice in causing these changes. An unknown number accommodated to this society which was dominated by white power centers, by seeking to be *assimilated* into the white society. Some did so by "passing" as Caucasians, others moved to areas where there were few or no other Negro families.

For years most white liberals and some Negro leaders, notably George Washington Carver, sought to improve the relationship between the races through *cooperation and collaboration*. Some of the most conspicuous monuments to this spirit of cooperation are the Jim Crow colleges scattered throughout the nation, and the settlement houses in the Negro ghettoes of large northern cities. The biracial character of these institutions can be seen in the Negro clientele, the white financial supporters, the biracial boards of directors, and the integrated staff.

More recently some advocates of change in this relationship have contended that *competition* is the best method of effecting change. Give the Negro the opportunity for a decent education, and he will be able to compete in the labor market. Give him equal opportunity at the ballot box, and the politicians in competing for his vote will abet change. Give the Negro an equal chance in employment and promotion practices, and he will be able to compete in the housing market for better homes, thus indirectly destroying the ghetto. Statements such as these have been uttered on countless occasions by the advocates of social change through competition.

The five largest Negro protest groups in the field of civil rights today illustrate the two major processes of achieving change. The two oldest, the NAACP and the Urban League, were founded and for decades relied primarily on *cooperation* as the process to be used in improving race relations. The three newest organizations—the Congress of Racial Equality, the Southern Christian Leadership Conference and the Student Nonviolent Coordinating

Committee—have placed a much greater emphasis on the use of conflict. By so doing they forced the Urban League and the NAACP to more militant positions which have involved occasional use of conflict.[7]

## The Change Agent

Any discussion of how planned social change is accomplished would be incomplete if limited only to the social processes involved. Frequently a part of the decision to make a deliberate effort to improve the social system includes engaging an outside specialist to help accomplish this change. Some years ago the staff of the National Training Laboratory adopted the very useful term, "change agent," to describe this outside specialist.[8]

Professional change agents can be found in all parts of society, and collectively they constitute one of the fastest growing categories of professional employment in American history. They include city planners, intergroup relations specialists, county agricultural agents, group workers, industrial and management consultants, executive secretaries of good government groups, labor union organizers, and a thousand other specialized vocations. This term could also include the pastor who is appointed or called to a certain church to see that a specific task, such as a

[7] For an excellent brief description of the changes in the approach to social change by the Negro protest groups see C. Eric Lincoln, *My Face Is Black* (Boston: Beacon Press, 1964). For a rationale for the shift to the conflict theory in the civil rights movement see Howard Zinn, *The Southern Mystique* (New York: Alfred A. Knopf, 1964).

[8] For a more detailed definition of the change agent and his role see Ronald Lippitt, Jeanne Watson, and Bruce Westley, *The Dynamics of Planned Change* (New York: Harcourt, Brace and World, 1958), pp. 10-14, 187-208, 226-38. For a very perceptive and persuasive analysis of the role of individuals in effecting social change see Richard T. LaPiere, *Social Change* (New York: McGraw-Hill Book Company, 1965). The author suggests three categories for change agents— innovators, advocates, and adopters.

building program or the integration of the congregation, is accomplished. It could include the growing number of urban work specialists who are appointed to denominational staff positions.

One of the more recent additions to this list of change agents is the community organizer, the person who seeks to help the residents and organizations of the community improve their relationships with the other social systems of society. To continue the two examples used earlier in this chapter, one type of community organizer would be the specialist employed by the Welfare Federation in the City of Glendale to help the businessmen and other leaders in South End develop the sense of common purpose which resulted in the creation of the nonprofit redevelopment corporation. Another type of community organizer is the civil rights leader who organized the Negro community to picket the board of education in Chicago in 1965.

The community organizer is the catalyst who tries to help the community identify its own problems, establish its own goals, and develop the procedures for realizing these goals. Frequently he will spend much of his time and effort in recruiting and training indigenous leadership. A successful community organizer eventually will work himself out of a job in that community.[9]

Inevitably the community organizer, and this is also true for nearly all other change agents, will discover that he must deal with the problem of power and the distribution of power. If he rejects the conflict theory of social change he will tend to stress a cooperative, or possibly a competitive, approach in the hope that the existing centers of power can be made more representa-

---

[9] For a clear and succinct description of the community organizer's responsibilities see Ross, *Community Organization,* pp. 200-211. For a more theoretical definition of the requirements of a good change agent see Ronald Lippitt, "Dimensions of the Consultant's Job" in *Journal of Social Issues,* XV, No. 2 [1959], 5-12.

tive of the total community and that his clientele will be able to gain a voice in these established power centers. Much of his time and energy will be spent in going back and forth between the community in which he is working (remember this may or may not be a geographical community) and the power structures located outside his community. He will concentrate on improving understanding, on opening and keeping open the channels of communication, on emphasizing areas of common agreement and minimizing areas of disagreements, and on nourishing good relations between his clientele and the outside community. As a result of these efforts he will become a highly visible person both inside and outside his community.

If the community organizer affirmatively accepts the validity and legitimacy of the conflict theory he is likely to advocate the creation of new centers of power. Instead of concentrating on the relationships *between* the community in which he is working and the external social systems, he will devote his efforts to working *within* the community. Generally he will be recruiting and training indigenous leaders, he will be helping to awaken and focus discontent, and he will emphasize the common objectives of the residents of the community. He will be working to develop strategies which will give the newly created power centers their maximum leverage. During these early stages of community organization he will be comparatively invisible to persons outside the community in which he is working.

## The Strategy of Intervention

Regardless of which theory of social change is accepted by the organizations and individuals interested in the community organization process, their efforts may be relatively ineffective unless they master the strategy of intervention.[10] This means careful and thoughtful selection of the time and place at which the effort is made to alter the course of events.

Should the protest against the lack of citizen participation in the urban renewal program be made just before the referendum is held on the bond issue to finance the project? Or should it be made during the mayoral race? Should the protest be directed to city hall or to the Urban Renewal Agency in Washington?

Should the Negro residents of the city seek to secure enactment of a fair housing ordinance by themselves? Or should they wait until the local council of churches comes out for this type of legislation and attempt to build a coalition with religious and other civic leaders? Should they press for this legislation during the election campaign or wait until the election is over?

Should the clergyman who is concerned about the newspaper strike which is in the ninth week attempt to settle it by offering to be a mediator between the union and management? Or should he attempt to organize a group of influential citizens who will investigate the dispute and then support one side in the controversy?

There are no simple universal answers to questions such as these. They do illustrate, however, the need for anyone interested in planned social change to carefully consider both timing

[10] For a detailed analysis of the strategy of intervention see Hans B. D. Spiegel, "Intervention Anyone?" in *Interracial News Service*, XXXIII [November-December, 1962], 1-5. The value of timing is extremely important in any effort to achieve change. Thus many political scientists contend that one of the vital characteristics of a great president is a sense of timing or knowing when and how to intervene in the legislative process. President Franklin Roosevelt's "court packing" plan of 1937 for changing the attitude of the Supreme Court toward New Deal legislation is an example of poor strategy of intervention. President Lyndon B. Johnson's television appeal for new legislation on voter registration following the beating of Negroes in Selma was an excellent example of timely intervention in the change process.

and the form of his intervention. His choice of strategy may be almost as important as his willingness to intervene.

With this brief introduction to the fundamental social processes, the role of the change agent, and the importance of strategic intervention, it is time to review the developments which have produced the contemporary concept of community organization.

Chapter Three

# The Evolution of an Idea

"The various charitable organizations in this city must get together and develop a systematic method of interagency communication. It is the only way we can reduce our vulnerability to the chiselers who are out to take advantage of us. Furthermore this would enable us to coordinate our efforts and use our resources more effectively." Comment of a settlement house worker in 1895.

"If the Great War taught us anything, it demonstrated the value of a cooperative financial campaign! Cleveland has had a joint fund raising drive for social welfare agencies since 1912. We need to get organized on a similar basis here." Comment of a board member of a social welfare agency in 1919.

"Community organization is more than the *field* which coordinates and promotes the work of many separate agencies, it is also a *process* through which problems are identified and solutions are developed." Comment of a social worker at a national conference in 1940.

"The only kind of foreign aid which is of any lasting value

today is the assistance which will help the people in underdeveloped areas help themselves." Comment of a critic of the United States' foreign aid program in 1955.

"The power structure in this town will continue to ignore us and our demands until that day when they see we have enough power to challenge their power. Then they'll listen." Comment of a civil rights leader in 1965.

These five comments illustrate the development of an idea which now bears the label "community organization." The evolution of this idea might be compared with a thread which has many strands. As new strands are added, the size, shape, and color of the thread changes. As it grows, it becomes stronger and can be used for many different purposes. This thread which is called community organization is woven from many strands, including the social work profession, partisan politics, the federal government, organized labor, religion, and the civil rights movement.

## Social Work Contribution

The largest and oldest strand in this thread has been contributed by social workers who coined the phrase and have produced the largest quantity of systematic studies, both theoretical and descriptive, on this subject.

Their contribution began back in the last third of the nineteenth century with the creation of scores of charitable agencies. Many of the early ones were created to help relieve the distress resulting from the devastation of the Civil War. For example, this was the era when scores of religious organizations responded to President Lincoln's call in his second inaugural address of March 4, 1865. "With malice toward none, with charity for all, with firmness in the right as God gives us to see the right, let us strive on to finish the work we are in, to bind up the nation's wounds, to care for him who shall have borne the battle and for his widow and orphan."

In response to this message, a response that was accelerated by the President's assassination a few weeks later, the people of America organized hundreds of orphanages, hospitals, and other charitable agencies. The 1880's saw the beginnings of the settlement house movement and a great increase in the agencies founded to help the immigrants from Europe. A quarter of a century after the close of the Civil War there were dozens of relief-giving agencies in every large city.

One inevitable result was a duplication of effort in certain "glamorous" fields and a comparative neglect of other areas of need. In addition, it was possible for unscrupulous individuals to seek and receive aid from several agencies at the same time while others in need were ignored.

Out of this chaotic scene came the realization that some form of cooperative effort was needed, and this was the beginnings of the first strand in the community organization thread. This first effort at community organization was the charity organization society movement. The first one was organized in Buffalo in 1877 followed by similar efforts the following year in New Haven, Boston, and Philadelphia. Cincinnati, Brooklyn, and Indianapolis joined the parade in 1879. The cooperating charitable agencies serving a given community organized to develop a central clearing house for the listing of all "cases" known to each. This reduced the chances for an individual client to exploit several agencies, and it also provided a structure for professional workers from several agencies to work together when each was helping the same family. In addition, the charity societies were able to work together on surveys to determine needs, to measure available resources, and to coordinate programs in a specific community.

The charity organization movement may have been premature and overly authoritarian as some later critics contend, and it did reduce its effectiveness by going into direct service programming; however, it also provided the base for the professionalization of social work, and it laid the foundations for the development of community organization as a field.[1]

The second phase of the evolution of this concept in the social welfare field began during the first decade of the twentieth century when the need for cooperative planning became apparent and resulted in an organizational structure known as the federation of social agencies movement. At first this was limited largely to planning, voluntary efforts at coordination of program, and operation of a central clearinghouse for information. Each agency continued its own separate fund raising drives. During World War I, however, cooperative fund raising drives were tried and .proved to be very successful and thus emerged the "community chest" concept. By the late 1920's more than three hundred cities had adopted this newest addition to the concept of community organization, and today the number of councils of social agencies exceeds six hundred.

Through the early 1930's the term "community organization" was being used by social workers to refer to a *field* of activity or a special area of administrative competence. The community organization specialist was the person who concentrated his efforts at promoting and coordinating the efforts of the various social

[1] This brief review of the historical evolution of community organization in social work is heavily dependent on the excellent account found in Campbell G. Murphy, *Community Organization Practice* (Boston: Houghton Mifflin Company, 1954) especially pp. 33-39. See also Steiner, *Community Organization;* Wayne McMillen, *Community Organization for Social Welfare* (Chicago: University of Chicago Press, 1945); Violet M. Sieder, "What Is Community Organization Practice in Social Work?" *The Social Welfare Forum* (New York: Columbia University Press, 1956), pp. 160-74.

agencies which were serving the people of a specific community. He worked with the institutions which served the people and seldom was in direct contact with the clients of the agencies.

New dimensions were added to the concept during the 1930's. These developments are summarized in the "Lane Committee" reports of 1939 and 1940. These reports were prepared by a committee of the National Conference on Social Welfare. Robert P. Lane, who was executive director of the Welfare Council of New York City was chairman of the committee.[2] The reports are extremely important for a variety of reasons.

First of all, the report of 1939 emphasized the concept of community organization as a *process* with which all social work is concerned (despite the unfortunate use of the word "field" in the title of the report). The committee recognized that community organization was *both a field and a process* which could be helpful in balancing needs against resources in social welfare activities. The report stated that community organization is concerned with the statement of needs, a definition of resources, and the continuing effort to keep these in proper adjustment while at the same time seeking to get at causes. Second, the committee recognized that the community organization process is not limited to the efforts of the social workers, but is carried on by religious, political, and other groups. Third, the Lane Report noted that within the social work profession community organization was beginning to stand out as a specialty comparable to casework and group work.

On the other hand the Lane Committee suggested that agencies concerned with community organization should not be involved

[2] "The Field of Community Organization," *Proceedings of the National Conference of Social Work, 1939* (New York: Columbia University Press), pp. 495-511. "Report of Groups Studying the Community Organization Process," *Proceedings of the National Conference of Social Work, 1940* (Columbia University Press), pp. 456-73.

in direct services to clients. In other words, the thinking reflected the older idea of coordination of the welfare agencies involved in direct service activities. It is also significant that the committee rejected terms and concepts such as social planning, social engineering, and social welfare planning. It is true that the Lane Reports marked the beginning of the modern history of community organization. It is also true that the members of the committee reflected some of the fears and worries of the business community of the 1930's. The Lane Reports were progressive, but they were not radical.

During the late 1940's other experts in the social work profession added important refinements to the community organization concept. The most important of these was the increasing preoccupation with strengthening the process by which a community makes decisions rather than upon the attainment of specific objectives. Kenneth Pray developed the concept of the community organizer as an "enabler" who works "with" the people of a community rather than "on" the community.[3] Wilbur Newstetter recognized the existence of a "natural" process of community organization which may or may not include the efforts of social workers.[4] Arthur Dunham argued for a broader definition of the role of the community organizer and pointed out that the most important responsibility of the community organizer often is to provide creative leadership.[5]

It is difficult to overemphasize the significance of these and

[3] "What Is Community Organization Social Work Practice?" *Proceedings of the National Conference of Social Work, 1947* (Columbia University Press), pp. 194-204.

[4] "The Social Intergroup Work Practice," *Proceedings of the National Conference of Social Work, 1947* (Columbia University Press), pp. 205-13.

[5] "What Is the Job of the Community Organization Worker?" *Proceedings of the National Conference of Social Work, 1948* (Columbia University Press), p. 168.

related contributions by other persons in the social work profession. As a result of their efforts, by about 1950 community organization was widely accepted as one of the three major fields of specialization in social work (the other two being case work and group work). During the 1950's the social workers continued to place great emphasis on process[6] and also on the responsibility of the community organization worker to help the community uncover and treat the causes of the problem which plagued the people. It was at this point in the evolution of community organization that a significant new effort was made to relate organization and planning. A book by Arthur Hillman pointed out the desirability of lifting community organization out of the social work context and tying it in to parallel efforts in planning, adult education, and other areas of cooperative endeavor.[7]

During the 1950's and the early 1960's many social workers became increasingly dissatisfied with older methods of rendering service to the disadvantaged and the inability of the welfare bureaucracy to solve the problems of the poor. As a result, in recent years social workers have become ardent champions of greater citizen participation and have sought to open up channels which would provide new opportunities for citizen initiative and responsibility.[8]

A major single contribution of the social work profession in the 1950's was the publication of Murray Ross's textbook.[9] Ross

[6] It is important to note here that the textbook on community organization by Wayne McMillen and published in 1945 was based on the concept that community organization was a process, not merely a field.

[7] *Community Organization and Planning* (New York: The Macmillan Company, 1950).

[8] Hillman, "Citizen Participation in Social Planning," *Social Progress Through Social Planning: The Role of Social Work* (New York: United States Committee of the International Conference of Social Work, 1964), pp. 33-38.

[9] *Community Organization.*

recognized the evolution of the concept of community organization. He noted the two foci for community organization: (1) the need to develop "meaningful functional communities" in the modern city so the individual may be able to develop a sense of belonging and feel that he is able to influence the events which shape his environment, and (2) the desirability of creating a sense of neighborhood in the several geographical areas which constitute a large metropolitan center.[10]

Ross also recognized and discussed the three major subgroups of community organization: (1) the "specific content" form which is a one-shot effort to achieve a single goal, and (2) the "general content" form which is usually an association of individuals or agencies—often run by an elite—that works to "reform" or improve a community, and (3) the process orientation which is less concerned about achieving specific objectives and more concerned with improving and enlarging the capacity of a community to function in respect to common problems.[11]

This definition of subgroups by Ross points up one of the most significant questions which the churchman who is interested in community organization should ask himself. "Am I primarily concerned with community organization as a method for reaching an objective, or am I primarily concerned with community organization as a process which will be useful in helping the people of this community plan for and influence social change?" The question does not have a "right" answer nor a "wrong" answer; however, the response given will determine how the person will react to the experiences and contributions of community development specialists, labor leaders, politicians, and civil rights leaders.

[10] *Ibid.*, p. 5.
[11] *Ibid.*, pp. 17-23.

## The Community Development Concept

Second in size only to the social work strand in the development of this thread is the strand bearing the label "community development." [12] While community organization owes its beginnings and much of its current strength to the social work profession, community development had a different set of ancestors.

Community development has grown out of the concern of professionals in the field of adult education who have sought a means of helping free people from the bonds of custom, tradition, and ignorance. The county agricultural agent, the extension worker from the state university, the field man for the farmers' cooperative, and the government representative from the Bureau of Indian Affairs are among the large number of change agents who have been advocates of community development through stirring up self-initiative. In foreign countries their counterparts include the agricultural missionary, the Peace Corpsman, the Point Four representative, and the technical consultant on loan from an American or European industrial firm.

Each of these change agents sees in the community development process a technique by which people living in a society bound by the chains of tradition can free themselves to take a new look at their problems and discover new methods of achieving a better

[12] For an excellent description of the similarities and differences between community organization and community development see Thomas D. Sherrard, "Community Development and Community Organization—Common Elements and Major Differences," *Rural and Urban Community Development in the United States of America* (New York: United States Committee of the International Conference of Social Work, 1962) pp. 9-18. For a more detailed statement of the values of community development, see William W. Biddle, *The Community Development Process* (New York: Holt, Rinehart and Winston, 1965). For an analysis of three case studies in the church's participation in community development see William H. Koch, Jr., *Dignity of Their Own* (New York: Friendship Press, 1966).

way of life. Perhaps the clearest definition of the goal of community development is that it places primary emphasis on human resource development and secondary emphasis on social change. As in community organization, in community development the emphasis is on helping people help themselves, but the means may differ. Community development workers stress the value of cooperation, usually seek to avoid conflict, expect to organize people around positive goals stated in positive terms, rather than discontent or conflict, and help to alter the attitudes of people toward change.

The differences between community organization and community development are many and varied. For example, in a severely blighted area the community organizer might attempt to rally the residents together to conduct a rent strike and thus force the landlords to improve the dwellings. The community development worker would stress a self-help formula and use a slogan such as, "You can live in a better neighborhood without moving," as the theme song of his organizing efforts. He would attempt to persuade the absentee owners to cooperate.

While this distinction is now disappearing, community development efforts have been limited primarily to rural areas, and the federal government, through the Department of Agriculture and other agencies, has been the major supporter of the technique. Community organization has been practiced almost exclusively in urban areas with practically no federal encouragement (the first major exception to this was Title II of the Economic Opportunity Act of 1964) and with the voluntary social welfare agencies the major sponsor.

The Christian who is interested in community development probably will emphasize the "love in action" theme and operate from a basic motivation of neighbor-centered love. He will be much more concerned with the improvement of persons through cooperation than the resolution of social problems through conflict.[18] His fellow Christian who sees community organization as the better technique will be more concerned with social justice and will argue that in this complex world the best expression of neighbor-centered love is to fight for social justice. He will be more concerned with accelerating the pace of social change than with the plight of the individual and likely will insist that the condition of the deprived individual can best be improved by altering the social structure. He will have far fewer reservations about the use of conflict, but will have major reservations about the effectiveness of cooperation.

Despite these differences, there are many similarities between the two specialties. Both rely on the intervention of professional change agents who are expected to help the people help themselves. Both anticipate that this will result in major changes in the ongoing social processes of the community. Both expect that it will result in a redistribution of power. Both believe that this is a dynamic process which will enable some individuals to come closer to realizing their God-given potential. Both depend upon the contributions of several disciplines to sharpen their methods of operation. Both assume that if the local people have the opportunity to establish the goals, the people will work hard to see that the goals are realized. Both emphasize the value of local self-determination and both recognize that this is not possible without broad participation. Both assume that the improvement of the individual and the improvement of the community are compatible and interdependent goals.

These similarities in goals, assumptions, and methodology mean that lessons learned by one are relevant to the other. The commu-

[18] For a good brief statement of the churchman's interest in community development see William W. Biddle, "Church and Community Development," *The Christian Century* (January 22, 1964), pp. 106-8.

nity development program has contributed three important insights which merit the attention of the churchman who is interested in the community organization process. The first of these is the heavy emphasis on human resource development, an emphasis far greater than is given to either influencing the course of social change or the acquisition of power. The second contribution is the experience in the use of cooperation, rather than conflict, in effecting social change. The third contribution is the support provided for the idea that the church can help the people in a community improve their lot. Community development has helped the church at large to see both the legitimacy and the urgency of the churches' involvement in human resource development and in social change.

## The Contributions of Politics and Labor

Perhaps the most faded strands in the community organization thread are the ones contributed by organized labor and politicians. One can trace these efforts at effecting social change through organized community efforts back to the Populists and the Wobblies (International Workers of the World) of the nineteenth century and through the current and far more sophisticated efforts of the union leaders such as Walter Reuther or political experts such as Ray Bliss.

Both organized labor and partisan politicians have been primarily concerned with organizational *methods* which would facilitate fulfillment of a specific goal such as securing a better wage contract or winning an election. Comparatively little attention has been devoted to the *process* through which a community of persons with common concerns goes about the defining and solving of problems. Despite this one-sided emphasis, labor and politics have learned four or five lessons from experience which are highly relevant to the whole community organization concept.

The most important of these is the value of the full-time professional organizer. Organized labor's power has grown as it has come to recognize the difference that a professional organizer can make in the organizing effort. The victory of John F. Kennedy in the 1960 presidential primaries illustrated the value of a well-staffed political organization. Today it is becoming increasingly apparent that competent professional staff is an essential part of an effective community organization effort.

In addition both labor leaders and politicians have demonstrated the utility of discontent in organizing a group of persons. Franklin D. Roosevelt rode to an overwhelming victory on a wave of discontent in 1932. Every major election sees one candidate seeking to rally the support of the "protest" vote of the persons who are discontented with the current state of affairs. Labor organizers have found discontent must be present if they expect to organize a nonunion plant. Conversely anti-union management often has recognized that a contented group of employees offers the best defense against the blandishments of the union organizer. Experts in community organization as diverse in their points of view as Murray Ross and Saul Alinsky have recognized that discontent is a basic ingredient in effective organization. It is the key motivation for any action-oriented effort.

A third lesson offered by the history of the American experience in labor and politics is the importance of developing coalitions in support of a particular issue. Too often beginners in community organization ignore history and seek to organize a single group and on that narrow base go out to influence the course of social change. The two master political figures of this century in America, Franklin D. Roosevelt and Lyndon B. Johnson, both recognized the importance of coalitions. The New

Deal was based on a coalition of the discontented, the dispossessed, the depressed, and the deprived. The presidential election of 1964 presented a coalition candidate against a candidate with a narrow partisan base. A notable illustration of the use of community organization for political purposes at the level of local government was in Kansas City during the tenure of L. P. Cookingham as city manager. Much of his support came from a coalition of neighborhood associations which he helped organize and staff. Labor became a power in American society with the organization of coalitions, first the Knights of Labor, then the American Federation of Labor, and later the Congress of Industrial Organizations. The power of a coalition of unions was multiplied when they formed a larger coalition with consumer groups, minority groups, or political parties. Rarely does the power of a single organization match the power of a coalition on any one issue. Coalitions do shift as the issues change and new alliances are put together. The community organizer who seeks to profit from history will recognize the necessity of understanding the dynamics of coalitions.

The fourth lesson might be called "the two-generation theory of conflict and reconciliation" and can be seen most clearly in the labor movement, although it also appears in the political arena. The organization of a new power bloc usually creates a sense of fear and insecurity in those who hold power and find that power threatened by a new organization. This often results in the creation of a gulf of distrust and alienation between the two parties that is so deep it extends beyond issues to personalities. Each side becomes convinced that the leaders of the opposition not only are wrong on the merits of the issue, but also are evil persons who cannot be trusted and are the kind of people with whom no decent Christian individual world freely associate.

The degree of alienation becomes so severe and the degree of distrust so great that personal reconciliation becomes extremely difficult if not impossible. It is not until a new generation of leaders comes along on both sides, or at least on the side of the controversy which was threatened by the emergence of the new power bloc, that reconciliation becomes possible and the leaders can view the issues apart from personalities.

Thus the personal relationships between the leaders of labor and management in the 1950's and 1960's has been far more amicable than were the relationships between their parents a generation earlier when the plant was first organized.

A similar development occurred in the national political arena where the Republican Party had been dominant for most of the seventy years following the election of Abraham Lincoln. In the 1930's a coalition, developed under the Democratic Party banner, threatened the power of the Republicans. Many of the older staunch Republicans found themselves unable to refer to the Democratic president except in terms which included a derogatory reference to his ancestry. A generation later their sons and daughters marched to the polls and voted for John F. Kennedy and Lyndon B. Johnson.

Some union leaders will insist that their experience adds a fifth lesson to this list. They will argue that the labor movement clearly demonstrates the value of conflict in developing and maintaining an organization strong enough to influence the course of social change and protect the interests of the members.

Their favorite example is the United Mine Workers union which freely resorted to the use of conflict in its early and middle years, and by 1947 the coal miners were the aristocrats of the labor movement in many respects including wage rates, fringe benefits, and political influence. These gains had been acquired through the use of conflict which often slipped over into the area of violence. The United Mine Workers union was a striking illustration of how rapid social change could be achieved through conflict.

In the late 1940's John L. Lewis, president of the UMW, switched tactics and began to cooperate with the mine owners in the mechanization of the industry. Fifteen years later the number of members of the UMW had dropped by fifty per cent, union welfare benefits had been reduced, several of the union-operated hospitals were closed or sold, and thousands of miners were irregularly employed in "doghole" mines for less than one-half the daily wage they had received in 1950.

Proponents of the mechanization program pointed out that cooperation had quadrupled the productivity of each miner. Many of the unemployed miners responded that the gains which had been achieved through years of bitter conflict began to disappear when the union began to cooperate with the mine operators.

While this is not the place to debate the causes of the unemployed coal miner's problems, the total range of experiences of the labor unions and political parties in America do offer some provocative insights for the churchman who is seriously interested in the dynamics of organization.

## The Civil Rights Movement

One of the newest and most colorful strands in the community organization thread is formed by the contribution of the civil rights movement. During recent years the organization of the struggle for racial equality has demonstrated three important lessons which are relevant to the community organization process.

By far the most important is the impact which a change in the value system of the "have nots" can have on the power of the "haves." The fight for freedom by the American Negro has been waged on several different fronts. Perhaps the most impressive gains have been won where Negroes were able to achieve a new dimension of freedom by adopting a new system of values.

For example, the freedom of the Negro sharecropper was severely limited so long as he was subject to coercive economic power of the white landlord. If he wanted to be able to get a loan of money or the seed for the new year's crops, he had to be careful to do nothing which might offend the man who owned the land and the local feed and grain store. Frequently this meant he could not register to vote because this might offend the local white power structure. When the Negro tenant adjusted his system of values so that the right to vote became more important than economic security, he broke the coercive power of the white landlord.

Likewise when the northern Negro councilman from the Negro ghetto changed his value structure so that the respect he was accorded by leaders in the civil rights movement became more important to him than his relationships with the white members of the city council, he also broke the power of coercion by which his white colleagues had limited his freedom. He now was less worried about winning and holding their respect and cooperation because he placed less value on these considerations. This freed him to oppose them on issues where earlier he would have cooperated because of fear of how the Caucasian councilmen might treat him if he failed to cooperate.

In both cases a reorientation of the values of the minority group member reduced the power of the majority power bloc. Thus when the tenant of a slum apartment ceases to be concerned about staying in the good graces of the landlord he becomes free to participate in a community organization venture which aspires to coerce the landlord into repairing his buildings.

A second contribution of the civil rights movement is that direct action often does work. This is not a new concept, but each generation has to learn many lessons for itself and today's generation of community organizers have been able to observe the successes of the Negro revolt and see both the advantages and the limitations of direct action. Nowhere else in this post-World War II world has the value of direct action been demonstrated so dramatically and so clearly.

More important is the third lesson of the contemporary civil rights movement. While many community organizers have contended that the only way to influence the course of social processes is through intervention with naked power, the civil rights movement has demonstrated that change can be accomplished by peacefully helping people have the opportunity to change their attitude and behavior. During the past decade thousands, perhaps millions, of white American citizens have changed their attitudes on the race question. These changes did not result from coercion, but rather because these Caucasians had the opportunity to know Negroes as persons and friends, to quietly discuss the problems of prejudice and discrimination, to bring the light of the Christian gospel to shine on their questions, and to grow in grace. This change in the viewpoints of white Americans has enabled the movement for racial equality to proceed at a far faster pace than could have been accomplished a decade earlier. Given the opportunity, some people may change their minds and readjust their value systems. In addition, this change in the social climate has meant that other persons have been "forced," through social and political pressures, to change their *behavior* even if they did not change their *attitudes*. It is difficult to overestimate the value of this lesson for Christians interested in the community organization process who might otherwise believe that the use of conflict is the only method of effecting social change.

## The Contributions of the Churches

One of the oldest strands in this thread, and perhaps the one which shows the greatest wear and tear, is drawn from the social gospel. In reacting to the papers presented at a conference on community organization, Shirley E. Greene commented, "This is where I came in." He went on to note that many of the suggestions that the churches and churchmen should participate in the community organization process, in the struggle for economic and political power, and in the pursuit of social justice are paralleled in the writings of Washington Gladden and Walter Rauschenbusch.

However, the Christian's concern for the oppressed and underprivileged goes back many centuries before the phrase "social gospel" was coined. It is an integral part of the gospel. Through the centuries it has been expressed in many ways, one of the latest being the churches' support for the civil rights movement. The march on Washington in 1963 and the Civil Rights Act of 1964 are striking illustrations of the churches' concern and of their influence.

The church has also been deeply concerned about the dignity of man, the imperative that each individual have the opportunity to realize his God-given potential and other goals which are a part of the community organization process.

Whether one thinks of community organization as a method of achieving social justice, of effecting social change, or as a *process* for the improvement of the individual, the social action wing of the Christian church clearly has made a major contribution.

A more specific contribution by the churches to community organization has been in the migrant ministry which increasingly has been concerned with the rights and dignity of the migrant laborers. One recent expression of this concern closely parallels many of the goals which are a part of the community organization process. "Mutual association with others is a basic need and right of all in a free society. . . . Forms of organization for democratic and self-determining participation in economic, political, civic and other areas of life and work, by which farm workers seek responsibly to advance their status will be encouraged." [14]

This is a clear expression of the churches' interest in both the goals and the process of community organization. The ministry to migrants supplies a long list of cases where the church not only has used the community organization process and methods to achieve these goals, but also has made significant contributions to the art.

## Urban Renewal and Citizen Participation

Earlier mention was made of the federal government's support of community development both at home and abroad. Another contribution of the federal government dates back to 1954 when the Housing Act of 1949 was amended to require each local public agency seeking financial help from the federal government in urban renewal to prepare a "workable program." The workable program consists of seven elements, one of which is citizen participation. The law requires that community organizations and individual citizens be involved in the planning, the discussion, and the evaluation of policy decisions for the local renewal programs. This is based on the assumption that there is a harmony of interest between the planners and the general public, between the holders of public power and the neighborhood residents, between those who may be forced to move by a re-

[14] "National Goals for the 5th Decade of Migrant Ministry 1960-1970" (New York: Division of Home Missions, National Council of Churches in Christ in the U. S. A., undated).

newal program and those who are responsible for helping them move.

After more than a decade of required citizen participation in urban renewal several lessons have been learned which contribute to the current state of the art of community organization.

Perhaps the most important is that it is possible for the citizen's advisory committee to be used by the public officials for their own ends. Experience has also demonstrated that it is very easy to put together an unrepresentative committee and very difficult to develop an effective and representative committee. It is also a very time-consuming process to develop an informed committee which can offer constructive suggestions. Urban renewal is a very complex operation. In addition, public officials frequently are subjected to considerable criticism for the delays which are unavoidable in the process, and they are reluctant to set up a committee which will create additional scheduling problems.[15]

It is ironic that the largest contribution of the citizen participation element of urban renewal, which was based on an acceptance of the cooperation theory of community organization, has been to provide nationwide impetus for the use of the conflict theory. The residents and leaders of an area which is to be subjected to renewal treatment have been using the workable program requirement for citizen participation as a club over

[15] For an excellent analysis of the implications of citizen participation in urban renewal see James A. Wilson, "Planning and Politics: Citizen Participation in Urban Renewal," *Journal of the American Institute of Planners*, XXIX, (November, 1963), 242-49. For a critical analysis from another perspective see Lyle E. Schaller, "Is the Citizen Advisory Committee a Threat to Rrepresentative Government?" *Public Administration Review*, XXIV (September, 1964), 175-79. A case study of an attempt to use community organization techniques in an urban renewal area is reported in *Adams-Morgan: Democratic Action to Save a Neighborhood* (Washington, D.C.: Office of Urban Renewal of the District of Columbia, 1964).

the heads of city officials. Frequently they will resort to the use of conflict in their efforts to gain a place at the drafting board where renewal plans are prepared. They insist that the law entitles, in fact requires, them to have such a place and that the official advisory committee is a farce and not at all representative of the residents of the area.

In effect, the 1954 amendment to the Housing Act of 1949 delineated the battleground and provided some of the weapons for several of the most significant recent efforts at community organization in urban America.

## Other Strands

Two other strands in this thread labeled community organization merit attention here, however, and the contributions of each are so clear that neither requires a detailed description. The first is the concept of nonviolent coercion. The late Mahatma Gandhi popularized the concept, and it is extremely important in community organization because it divides the persons who support the use of conflict in achieving social change into two distinct groups. The first recognizes the value of conflict in the social process but is unwilling to move over the line which separates conflict from violence. The second is willing to resort to the use of violence.

The discipline or art of group dynamics is the other important strand which must be recognized in any analysis of the major contributors to the art and process of community organization. The insights contributed by the specialists in this field often may be crucial in determining whether an attempt at community organization will result in the effective participation or the mere manipulation of the residents of a neighborhood.

Out of this varied assortment of experiences have emerged several assumptions and principles which constitute the basic foundation for most of the current activities in community organization. These include the acceptance of community organization as a dynamic process based on the assumption that people do have the capacity to define and solve their own problems, the belief that self-imposed changes and self-defined goals have more meaning for the individual than those imposed by outsiders, the importance of the professional change agent in this process, the value of discontent as the key motivation for action, the necessity of recruiting and training indigenous leaders, the importance of coalitions in influencing the decision-making process, the assumption that the basic goals of the community organization process are compatible with and supportive of democratic principles, and the need for a redistribution of power if the pace of social change is to be accelerated.

Among the professional workers in community organization there is widespread agreement on all of the above assumptions and principles. The consensus breaks down very quickly, however, when the conflict theory of social change is added to the list. While many community organizers contend that the rejection of the use of conflict is naive and unrealistic, others argue that it is inappropriate for the Christian who preaches an ethic of love or the church which was founded on the expression of God's love for man to resort to the use of conflict. The result is a major conflict over the use of conflict.

Chapter Four
_____

# Conflict over Conflict

"Why do the labor unions insist on striking? Even if they do get higher pay, they'll never make up what they have lost in wages while they have been out on strike." Comment of a minister in 1937.

"When they (the civil rights groups) began to picket the schools here and thus endangered the safety of small children, they set race relations back at least ten years in this town." Comment of a clergyman in a northern city in 1964.

"How can a Christian minister, who preaches a doctrine of love, engage in the violence which has been a part of the race revolution?" Comment of the lay leader of a church whose minister marched in a picket line in 1963.

"The church of Jesus Christ can never approve or condone the use of violence, nor can it ever be a part of any movement which uses conflict to achieve its goals. The end never justifies the means!" Comment of a Chicago clergyman in 1962 in response to a request that his church become a member of a community organization effort.

These comments are representative of the reactions of many Christians to the use of conflict in the process of achieving social change.

As the result of the confluence of two major trends—the growing acceptance of conflict as the most effective means of achieving social change and the growing interest of church men in the community organization process—this matter of the Christian's use of conflict has become the crucial issue in any discussion of the church's involvement in community organization.[1]

Before moving to a discussion of the reasons for the increased use of conflict in the community organization process and the dilemma this has created for the committed Christian, it may be helpful first to define terms, and then to examine the advantages and disadvantages attributed to the use of conflict.

## What Is Conflict?

Conflict is the clash of differing points of view. A century ago Marx and other theorists used the word "conflict" to describe the violent clash of irreconcilable interests, loyalties, values, or opinions. Today the term is also used to describe more moderate differences of opinion or values. Some scholars contend that "social tension" is a more useful term than is the word "conflict." Social tension, or conflict in this more moderate sense, is an ever present element of the world and always exists among the or-

[1] The fundamental issue of conflict is far larger and much older than the concept of community organization. Some of the most advanced thinking on the subject is being done by students of international relations and scholars in the behavioral sciences. For an example of this see Roger Fisher, ed., *International Conflict and Behavioral Science: The Craigville Papers* (New York: Basic Books, 1964). For the classic statement in American political history on conflict see *The Federalist Papers* (New York: Washington Square Press, 1964), pp. 16-24. An excellent brief statement from a sociological perspective is Rolf Dahrendorf, "Toward a Theory of Social Conflict," Etzioni, *Social Change,* pp. 89-111.

ganizational units of society. Conflict does not exist apart from competition; however, there are many levels of conflict ranging from very friendly competition to violence. In the community organization process one can distinguish three distinct forms of conflict. The first is the social tension which is present even in cooperative efforts to achieve a consensus. The second is the more visible, open, and active nonviolent form of conflict which may include picketing, strikes, election campaigning, passive resistance, and nonviolent civil disobedience. The third form is violence and includes coercion, blackmail, or the use of force. In each form and at each level the element of competition is present, however.[2]

Conflict may result in social change, or it may accelerate the pace of change. On the other hand, change often occurs without conflict, and conflict does not always produce change.

The church has always been involved in conflict, and so the question of the use of conflict by churchmen is not a new issue. The church has always been in conflict with sin, evil, and injustice. The freedom God has given man means that man often finds himself in conflict with God. Conflict is a central theme in scores of hymns.

The problem with the use of conflict in community organization is twofold. First of all, there is always the risk that nonviolent conflict will spill over into violence. When conflict is used as a technique of achieving social change, it is necessary to maintain the momentum of the conflict until change begins to occur. Thus the Negro leaders in Alabama in early 1965 had to maintain

[2] For a very helpful definition of conflict in this context see LaPiere, *Social Change*, pp. 478-81. For an excellent analysis of the place of conflict in the development of controversy, see James S. Coleman, *Community Conflict* (New York: The Free Press of Glencoe, 1957). For a most provocative analysis of conflict as a factor in group formation see Georg Simmel, *Conflict and the Web of Group Affiliations* (New York: The Free Press of Glencoe, 1955).

the momentum of demonstrations after President Johnson had asked for a voting rights bill and until Congress acted. During this effort to maintain the momentum of conflict there always are many opportunities for the conflict to become violent.

The second risk in the use of conflict is that it may produce unexpected results. Instead of accelerating the pace of change, it may produce severe repercussions. The use of conflict by anti-communists in communist nations is a striking example, but the same reaction also may occur when community organizers resort to the use of conflict in a democracy. The response by police officers in both the North and the South to the nonviolent protests of Negroes is but one example. Perhaps this is inevitable at times. This is certainly not the primary goal, however. The primary purpose of conflict in community organization is to apply leverage against the established power centers of society and thus change the idealogical position of the opponent. The purpose is not to create violence, but violence may be a part of the total action-reaction process.[3] This raises the obvious question: May the Christian engage in nonviolent conflict when this may result in a violent response by those resisting change? At what point does the Christian stop applying leverage because of a probable violent reaction? On the other hand, may the Chris-

[3] See the article by Martin Luther King, "Behind the Selma March," *Saturday Review,* April 3, 1965, in which Dr. King suggests that the use of violence against the protestors is an integral part of a four-step process by which Negroes use conflict (in the form of demonstrations) to achieve change through legislation. For a helpful statement on how nonviolent action can be used to secure change see William Robert Miller, *Nonviolence: A Christian Interpretation* (New York: Association Press, 1964). Perhaps the best book on the role of the Christian in conflict situations and the process of nonviolent resistance is Harvey Seifert, *Conquest by Suffering* (Philadelphia: The Westminster Press, 1965). An extremely relevant brief discussion of conflict is "When Christians Disagree: The Role of Controversy in the Church," *Social Action,* Vol. XXIX (February, 1963).

tian resort to the use of violence in attempting to apply the leverage necessary to effect change?

## Arguments Favoring the Use of Conflict

The first, and most obvious, argument in support of the use of conflict as a technique for organizing a community and for accelerating the pace of social change *is that it usually works.* While many will criticize the means and others will object to the ends, no one can deny that the use of conflict does cause men to rally to the cause, and that it does hasten change. History is full of examples. Two hundred years ago the Tories argued that an attitude of cooperation and accommodation with England was the best policy for the American colonies to choose. The radicals of the day, such as Samuel Adams, Patrick Henry, and others, were less reluctant to use conflict, and their view prevailed. As a result the colonies achieved a greater degree of freedom at a more rapid pace than they would have under a policy of cooperation. (It should be added that the changes resulting from the use of conflict frequently turn out to be radically different than the goals originally articulated by those who encouraged the use of conflict.)

The American labor movement has placed heavy reliance upon the use of conflict, and, while many contemporary observers argued that it was a costly choice, wage levels increased more rapidly and working conditions improved at a faster pace in the unionized factories than in the nonunion shops. The average production worker who is a union member will earn more money in a month, year, or lifetime than will the average worker who is not a union member. The difference will far exceed the amount of money spent for union dues or lost because of strikes. In addition, he will enjoy a higher level of benefits after he retires.

Despite the reservations and objections of many churchmen, such as those represented by the opening paragraphs of this chapter, the conflict theory usually works. It has worked for the native leaders in Africa and Asia who sought to hasten the decline of European colonialism. It has worked for the ghetto resident in urban America who sought to halt the bulldozers of urban renewal. It has worked for the segregationists of the South who attempted to break the ties of their region with the Democratic Party. It has worked for the American Negro who recently concluded that conflict is superior to cooperation or accommodation in achieving change in the civil rights field. It has worked in hundreds of other instances where a relatively small group of individuals sought to change the social order.

A second advantage of the use of conflict is that it may help to sharpen the issues and enable people to distinguish more easily between two different points of view. One method of using conflict to clarify differences of opinion is a debate. When a controversial issue is described by one speaker, the various facets of the subject may not come through to the audience as clearly as when different viewpoints are presented in a debate. An excellent example of how conflict sharpens the issues and reveals new facets of a problem can be found in the history of the conflict between organized labor and management. Scores of social ills which previously had been overlooked were revealed in this conflict.

For conflict to exist there must be a sharp divergence of viewpoints and value judgments. On the other hand the processes of cooperation, accommodation, and assimilation by definition seek to minimize differences and gloss over varying points of view. Whenever two or more solutions are offered for a single social problem, tension usually is present. Efforts to reduce this tension often tend to confuse the issue. Conflict heightens the tension, provides an impetus for critical examination, and supplies a floodlight of publicity which exposes the issues for study by all interested persons. Thus conflict has great social utility in helping the individual citizen choose among alternatives. (Critics of this view contend that conflict may be used to disguise or conceal the real issues and result in the substitution of false, misleading, or irrelevant issues.)

A third advantage of conflict is that it can be a creative force when properly used. The man most widely associated with the use of conflict in community organization, Saul Alinsky of the Industrial Areas Foundation, argues, "Controversy has always been the seed of creation."[4] Alinsky insists that the use of conflict can be justified, not only because it works, but also because it provides the most fertile ground for creative thinking.

Historical evidence is overwhelmingly on Alinsky's side on this point, for conflict not only produces compromises, it also yields new ideas which might not have been conceived without the stimulus of conflict. An endless number of illustrations could be cited ranging from the theological contributions of Martin Luther to the wartime development of radar, and from the prophecies of Daniel, Hosea, and Amos to the technological advances resulting from the competitive conflicts of American capitalism.

An argument more relevant to the subject of community organization is the fact that the use of conflict has been an extremely effective method of obtaining a seat at the bargaining table for the disfranchised. When the labor unions resorted to the use of conflict in the 1930's, they gained a seat at the table where

[4] Quoted in Stephen C. Rose, "Saul Alinsky and His Critics," *Christianity and Crisis,* XXIV (July 20, 1964), 145.

the decisions on wages, hours, and working conditions were made. When Negro mothers picketed the public schools a quarter of a century later, they gained a voice in the review of the policies which had produced half-day classes and segregated schools. When the poor rebelled against the development of new welfare programs by the local power structure in the mid-1960's, their protests were heard in Sargent Shriver's office, and they gained a voice in planning the poverty program. Dozens of other examples could be cited to show how the use of conflict has enabled the protesters to be heard when community decisions were being made.

It is instructive to note that several organizations which were founded on an acceptance of the use of conflict did win a seat at the bargaining table at least in part because of their willingness to resort to conflict. Once they had won this seat, however, they abandoned the use of conflict and began to emphasize the use of cooperation and the building of a consensus. Is, perhaps, the main value of conflict in community organization to gain recognition for a previously disfranchised group, rather than to influence subsequent decisions?

Conflict is also useful in overcoming the blight of institutionalism. Most institutions—government agencies, business corporations, school systems, civil rights organizations, political parties, and religious bodies—tend to become conservative as they grow older. They also tend to become increasingly irrelevant as the social order changes. Conflict is a common method of overcoming this form of institutional blight.

Often the conflict is internal. It may be a proxy fight in an industrial corporation which brings in a new board of directors and a new management team or frightens the old board and old officers into pursuing a more dynamic course of action. It may be an internal struggle to replace the national chairman of a political party overwhelmed by the opposition in a major election.

Sometimes the conflict is external. A new and more militant civil rights group may be formed because the existing ones appear to be too conservative. A Protestant denomination, which heretofore has limited its operations to the South, may move into the North because it believes its northern counterpart is not sufficiently aggressive in evangelism and new church development.

The forms vary greatly, but conflict is perhaps the most widely used device to overcome institutional inertia. Occasionally it fails, but usually it yields at least some beneficial results.

A sixth advantage of conflict is that it often stimulates participation in the decision-making process by persons who either have dropped out of an active role or have always been passive. In the presidential election of 1960 the conflict over the candidacy of a Roman Catholic brought out a record number of voters. If one accepts the principle that the democratic process works best when the maximum number of persons participate, then the use of conflict is valuable because it does stimulate participation by those who otherwise would be inactive.

Finally there are those who argue that conflict is a beneficial element in the social process because conflict almost invariably results in a shift in the distribution of power. The advocates of this position contend that the redistribution of power not only offers the benefits of rejuvenating social institutions and providing seats for newcomers at the bargaining table, but also that it yields other more general salutory consequences and stimulates changes in all facets of the social order. A distant relative of this argument is Thomas Jefferson's contention that every generation needed to experience its own revolution for the general good of the nation.

If the use of conflict has all these advantages,[5] how can any Christian argue against the use of conflict in community organization and in effecting social change? What is the basis for the conflict over the use of conflict?

As is true in so many areas of social action, there are two sides to this issue. The use of conflict in achieving social change and in promoting the community organization process is fraught with risks—and the risks are especially severe for those who do not recognize the disadvantages that are inherent in the conflict theory.

## Arguments Against the Use of Conflict

Some of the professionals in the social work field contend that the greatest drawback to the use of conflict in the community organization process is that it provides a temporary stimulus which may prevent the development of a permanent foundation for participation. While the use of conflict does attract some persons who might not otherwise become involved in the community organization process, it also repels others who find conflict to be very distasteful. Most American citizens habitually prefer peace, harmony, and a spirit of cooperation to the turmoil and disharmony which usually accompany the use of conflict.

In addition, the use of conflict frequently means that the interest of both leaders and followers tends to be focused on a single issue. When that issue disappears or ceases to be controversial, the whole organization collapses. It is quite possible for the use of conflict to create a situation *which appears to have*

[5] For a discussion of other advantages of conflict not directly related to community organization see Martin E. Marty, "Epilogue: The Nature and Consequences of Social Conflict for Religious Groups," *Religion and Social Conflict* (New York: Oxford University Press, 1964), pp. 173-93. An extremely useful examination of the positive functions of conflict can be found in Lewis Coser, *The Functions of Social Conflict* (New York: The Free Press of Glencoe, 1956).

*produced active participation by indigenous leaders.* However, when the outside organizers who have stimulated the conflict leave the scene, the excitement which brought out the local participants fades away and the community soon lapses back into apathy. This also illustrates a very important point in the theory of social change; it is possible to have social motion without achieving social change.

When it becomes apparent that the effort has not produced indigenous leaders who possess both the willingness and the ability to follow through in the community organization, then the organizers may be tempted to create conflict, *simply for the sake of conflict and without regard for the real issues,* in order to rearouse the interest of the residents and thus draw them back into participation. If conflict is used to stimulate the residents to organize, the temptation will be ever-present to create artificial conflict merely to preserve the existence of the neighborhood council. This not only is a perversion of the community organization process, it also will eventually be self-defeating. The legend of the boy who cried wolf too often provides an appropriate moral.

A second objection to the use of conflict grows out of the increasing degree of alienation in American society. The social observer in America sees a nation with a widening gulf between the "haves" and the "have nots," a land where racial segregation is still the dominant theme in residential neighborhoods, in the church, and in most of the institutional structures; a country where geographical compartmentalization emphasizes the social, economic, cultural, and political divisions.

Thus critics of the conflict theory have an impressive foundation for their argument that the Lord is calling every church and every Christian to be a reconciling agent and that every action and activity of both the congregation and the individual must be performed in a spirit of love. The role of the church in this age of alienation is to serve as a channel for God's reconciling love as it flows from God to man to his brother. Clearly there is little room for the use of conflict in this argument. On the other hand it can be argued that in many times and places neighbor-centered love *requires* the Christian to resort to the use of conflict.

Perhaps the most important objection to the free use of conflict in community organization is made by persons who understand and accept the value of conflict in effecting social change. They acknowledge that the church has had to use conflict to achieve many desirable changes both in the social order in general and also within the institutional forms of the church. These same persons are reluctant, however, to give unreserved approval to the use of conflict in the community organization process. They recognize that conflict can easily turn into violence, that it can be very destructive, and that it readily moves from nonviolent protest to a disruption of public order. They remember how the careless use of conflict made many liberal organizations highly vulnerable to communist infiltration during the past several decades. They are well aware of how conflict situations can be subverted to play into the hands of communist agitators. (But there is also the risk that an uncritical acceptance of this argument means that the cry "Communist" is always available as a handy weapon by those who resist social change.)

In addition to their concern about the use of communist tactics and the dangers of communist infiltration, these objectors often are even more concerned about the temptations and pitfalls which lie ahead of the churchman who unreservedly accepts the conflict theory of social change. They fear he may find the excitement and the acquisition of power heady medicine and may become vulnerable to the corrupting influences of power. He may seek to generate conflict largely for the excitement of conflict itself. He may quickly move from using conflict for constructive purposes to the use of conflict for the preservation of his own position of leadership. He may turn to the use of conflict as a tool for the destruction of legitimate opposition.

Basically these objectors are not opposed to the use of conflict. They do contend, however, that conflict is a powerful weapon which should be reserved for the use of experienced, mature, and responsible leaders lest it destroy democratic values and needlessly hurt individuals.

Perhaps the best recent illustration of this type of objection to the conflict theory can be found in the white man's attitude toward the movements for national independence in Africa. The same attitude is often expressed by older persons in established positions of institutional leadership in agencies seeking social change such as labor unions, denominational agencies, and civil rights organizations. (There is a disconcertingly strong resemblance between those who advocate this position and those who contend that the "younger generation" is not yet ready to assume the responsibilities of leadership and authority.)

Another, and much more categorical, argument against the conflict theory is offered by the veterans of community development operations who favor cooperation as the best method of achieving social change.[6] The Christian doctrine of man deemphasizes the distinctions of race and class which are the trademarks of a sinful society. The cooperative approach stresses the ability of man to solve his problems through rational procedures. It is based upon the premise that because he is created in the

---

[6] An excellent brief on behalf of cooperation and the role of consensus is offered by University of Chicago professor Philip C. Hauser, "Conflict vs. Consensus . . . ," *Chicago Sun-Times,* December 13, 1964. For a more detailed exposition of this point of view see Biddle, *The Community Development Process.*

image of God, man does have the ability to transcend his own selfish interests and to make decisions which are in the best interests of the total community.

Thus, contend these people, the only appropriate position for the Christian interested in the community organization process is to renounce the use of extreme forms of conflict, which can be justified only on the grounds that man is a sinner who is more likely to respond to coercion than to love, and to seek to operate on the higher plane of love and brotherhood. This type of objection to conflict has been developed in its most sophisticated form by Christian pacifists.

This argument is given further support by those who contend that the Christian interest in the community organization process should be based, *not on the goal of social change, but rather on the goal of helping each human being realize the full potential of his God-given ability*. They contend that while the use of conflict may have a favorable influence in achieving that goal, the deleterious effects of conflict more than offset the beneficial effects.

Perhaps the most important philosophical argument against the use of conflict is based on the ancient question of ends and means. Does the end justify the means? The traditional Christian response is no. Is it possible for a "bad" method to produce a "good" end? If mild conflict turns into violence, and violence turns into hate, will the end product be corrupted by the means used to achieve that end? These are vital moral questions to which the Christian must address himself before resorting to the use of conflict.

A sixth argument against the use of conflict is that it may result in the identification of the wrong enemy. An adverse reaction to a proposed urban renewal project develops into an attack on the planners and politicians in city hall rather than into an attack on the causes of blight and decay. It is easier to denounce the planners and politicians than it is to determine the causes of slums. Similarly dissatisfaction with the welfare policies of the city or county turns into ridicule of those who administer those policies rather than into an examination of the causes of poverty or the legislative pressures which established those policies. A new attempt to organize a community may be built around a destructive attack on the existing organizations and agencies which serve the residents rather than around a constructive program to solve the social problems of that neighborhood.

In each of these illustrations, and they are representative illustrations, the pressure to identify the source of the problem in simple and easily understandable terms often may result in focusing discontent on the wrong point in the social order. This not only engages the wrong enemy in conflict, it also may permit the right enemy to continue his work without interruption while potential allies are busy fighting one another. In addition, it greatly inhibits creative community planning and goal formation.

## Why Use Conflict?

If the use of conflict raises so many questions and objections, why have churchmen turned increasingly to the conflict theory of achieving social change?

A variety of answers could be offered to this question, but three stand out above all others.

1. As a person becomes more active in pursuing a specific goal, he is likely to become more concerned with the end and less concerned with the means than when he is discussing ethical considerations in more abstract terms. In the battle for racial equality most of those who raised ethical questions about the use of sit-ins, picketing, and economic boycotts were persons standing outside the struggle. During organized labor's struggle for recognition of the principle of collective bargaining most of those who

offered ethical objections to the use of strikes, boycotts, and picketing were not actively involved in labor's struggle.

The same situation prevails in the field of community organization today. Those who are most intimately involved in using the community organization process as a means of achieving social justice have the fewest reservations about the use of conflict. *In this struggle, as in the labor movement and the civil rights battle, the weapons are chosen by those who are engaged in the fighting, not by the observers on the sidelines!*

2. During the past several years a large proportion of the churchmen and their advisers who have been active in community organization have been persons who accepted the conflict theory. Thus a self-validating and self-perpetuating cycle was established.

3. The conflict theory is psychologically compatible with the personality characteristics of the activist—and it is from the activists among churchmen that are drawn the leaders and the followers in the community organization process. The use of conflict usually produces excitement, headlines, a sense of movement, a clear personification of the enemy, and some measure of immediate achievement.

## The Dilemma

This conflict over the use of conflict has created a major dilemma for the committed Christian who recognizes that the community organization process can be a valuable means both for promoting social justice and for the development of human resources. On the one hand, he wants to act in a spirit of love and reconciliation toward each of his neighbors, on the other hand, he sees that the use of conflict often is the most effective method for organizing a community and for achieving social change. He discovers that the best known churchmen in the field of community organization accept the conflict theory. He finds that the most widely publicized efforts in community organization have been based on acceptance of conflict. He sees that the use of conflict often does result in a redistribution of power, and he recognizes that many of the dispossessed and disfranchised must gain the feel of power before they can be expected to participate actively in the process of making community decisions.

He may be able to work his way out of this dilemma by systematically evaluating his goals, the priorities of these goals, his purpose in participating in the community organization process, and the urgency of his own concern. Gradually, however, he finds himself moving toward acceptance of a method which is not wholly compatible with his Christian ideals. This is the dilemma in which countless churchmen have found themselves as they struggle with the issue of their own participation in the community organization process. They are committed to acting in a spirit of love, but they also are earnest seekers after that elusive goal of social justice. There is no simple way out of this dilemma.

One Presbyterian minister who has been very active in community organization and who also places great emphasis on the importance of reconciliation, described his response to this dilemma in these terms:

Before even beginning to develop tactics and approaches related to a man or agency which might create more tension, or an open conflict relationship, I would make every effort to meet the person or persons and explain what kind of cooperation is needed from them and why. I would try first to get their assent, agreement, or willingness to cooperate fully. If they then refuse, or become indignant (which is more often the case), or later break their side of an agreement (which is many times the case), then the pressure of larger group action becomes appropriate. It's a matter of negotiating with the dignity of equals—reconciliation through equal power at the bargaining table. But the personal, direct approach should always be made first.

Regardless of his own resolution of this dilemma, it is important for every churchman to recognize that other Christians, equally committed to the causes of social justice and human resource development, may come out with a different answer to this question over the use of conflict. Nowhere in America is this division of opinion among Christians over the use of conflict in community organization better illustrated than in Chicago where it has developed into a major controversy.

Chapter Five

# Controversy over Controversy

"From a theoretical point of view I find Alinsky's methods leave a lot to be desired, but they do work! The only successful community organization efforts in Chicago have been those of the Industrial Areas Foundation. I'm enough of a pragmatist to support something that works, if it is the only way to solve the problem. Until someone else comes along with a better method of community organization, I'll support Alinsky, and I'll urge my friends in other cities to do likewise."

With this comment a prominent denominational executive in Chicago summed up one Protestant position in what has become the most controversial story of community organization in America.

The story begins back in 1938 when Saul D. Alinsky, who began his professional life as a criminalogist in Joliet State Prison, helped to organize the Back of the Yards Neighborhood Council in Chicago's slaughterhouse district. The Back of the Yards was an overwhelmingly Catholic working class neighborhood which was changed, through the community organization process, from a blighted and disorganized area into a stable community. It soon began to receive widespread publicity as a "model" of what could be accomplished through community organization.[1] (It must be added that experts in community organization today seldom point to Back of the Yards as a model; they contend it is now an anachronism because of the religious and ethnic homogeneity of the area. Others wonder if part of its success rests on the effectiveness of the community in keeping Negroes out and maintaining the all-white character of the neighborhood.)

Out of this effort of Alinsky's came two significant by-products. One was the Industrial Areas Foundation (IAF) which was organized in 1940 in response to requests from across the country for help and advice in solving community problems. By mid-1964 the IAF had responded to forty-four requests in several states for assistance and had received approximately $1,750,000 in gifts, grants, and fees. Most of the ventures by the IAF into community organization involved working with Spanish-speaking groups in the western states. An inconclusive effort in Lackawanna, New York and a well publicized defeat in Chelsea in New York City accounted for most of Alinsky's work east of the Mississippi River until 1959 when he came back into Chicago. During 1964 and 1965 Alinsky received invitations from church groups in Detroit, Buffalo, Kansas City, Syracuse, Rochester, and other cities to come in and describe his methods. In several cities contracts were entered into between the IAF and the local group in which the IAF agreed to come and help organize a community.

The second by-product of the Back of the Yards experience was

---

[1] For a sympathetic description of the Back of the Yards Council see Martin Millspaugh and Gurney Breckenfeld, *The Human Side of Urban Renewal* (New York: Ives Washburn, 1960), pp. 177-219.

the publication of his book on community organization in which Alinsky described the role of the "radical" in perpetuating democracy in America.[2] The book is an impassioned account of the "people's organizations" in which "the people" gain the power to control their own destiny. This volume has become the primer for both the supporters and the critics of Alinsky's method of community organization.

In the 1950's Alinsky began a new series of efforts in Chicago which have received tremendous publicity, especially within church circles. At first Alinsky served as a consultant to the Chicago archdiocese of the Roman Catholic Church as Catholic leaders sought to work more effectively among Puerto Ricans in the city. This long, close relationship between Alinsky and the Chicago archdiocese has led some observers to conclude that the IAF is a "tool" of the Roman Catholic Church. The allegation has been denied as ridiculous by both Roman Catholic and Protestant clergymen in Chicago as well as by Alinsky himself.

Later, in 1959, a group of Protestant and Roman Catholic clergymen and business leaders contracted with the IAF to organize a community in southwestern Chicago. In May, 1959, after four months of surveying and planning by the staff of the IAF, the Provisional Organization for the Southwest Community was established. In August the IAF withdrew, and the permanent organization for the Southwest Community (OSC) was constituted in October, 1959. Two years later it included 137 local institutions as members and employed five staff members with a budget of $50,000. Eleven Roman Catholic parishes and approximately one half of the fifty-plus Protestant churches in the area affiliated with the OSC, and several clergymen have been among the most active leaders. By 1960 a Protestant caucus was estab-

[2] *Reveille for Radicals* (Chicago: The University of Chicago Press, 1964).

lished so that a "Protestant position" could be presented and supported in the annual meeting.

From the very beginning the OSC benefited from large contributions from the churches and continues to depend on the churches for a large share of its financial support. It has also been caught up in the race battle, and at various times in its brief life has been charged with being both a segregationist and an integrationist operation.

The second, and by far the best known, of the recent efforts by the IAF to organize a community in Chicago occurred in Woodlawn, an area just south of the University of Chicago. Once an all-white middle-class neighborhood, Woodlawn became an overwhelmingly Negro community during the 1950's. Racial tensions were increased by the plans of the University of Chicago to acquire additional land and raze the buildings for campus expansion just south of the Midway. Implementation of this plan would require relocation of scores of Negro families.

At this point in history Alinsky received an invitation from the Woodlawn Pastors' Alliance to present his ideas on community organization. In several meetings and in a lengthy memorandum Alinsky explained his methods of organization. After much discussion in the spring of 1959, the IAF was invited to submit a specific proposal. Next came the effort to raise the necessary funds. A grant of $21,000 was made by the United Presbyterian Board of National Missions, $69,000 came from the Schwarzhaupt Foundation of New York, and a $50,000 donation was made by the Roman Catholic Archdiocese of Chicago. The Temporary Woodlawn Organization was formed in 1960 and soon was replaced by a permanent organization which also bore the initials TWO.[3]

[3] For a very sympathetic account of the history and work of TWO, see Charles E. Silberman, *Crisis in Black and White* (New York: Random House, 1964),

The Woodlawn Organization, like OSC, involved a number of churches, both Protestant and Roman Catholic, from the very beginning. It also was caught up in a storm of controversy. From a denominational point of view the United Presbyterian Church in the U.S.A. consistently supported the effort in Woodlawn. In other Protestant groups, partly because of polity and partly because of the lack of a national policy, the decision on participation was left to the individual congregations. Some churches were active participants from the beginning, some came in later, others stayed out completely, and a few withdrew after originally being a part of TWO. In 1965 churches from a dozen Protestant denominations were represented in TWO.

In April, 1961, five pastors withdrew from the Woodlawn Pastors' Alliance in protest against the use of community organizers by IAF whose "organizing tactics are based on the cultivation of fear, hatred, and usable antagonism." [4] The community newspaper, which was an ardent supporter of TWO in the early days, later turned into a bitter critic and repeatedly emphasized the fact that the leaders of TWO did not live in Woodlawn.

----

pp. 317-55. See also Jane Jacobs, "Chicago's Woodlawn—Renewal by Whom?" *Architectural Forum*, May, 1962, pp. 122-24; Ruth Moore, "Woodlawn: An Urban Battlefield," *Chicago Sun-Times*, April 9, 1961; Georgie Anne Geyer, "Woodlawn: A Community in Revolt," *Chicago Scene*, III, No. 12, 12-17; Robert M. Davidson, "If Justice Is the Goal—Organize," *Social Action*, February, 1965, pp. 5-14; Ulysses B. Blakely and Charles T. Leber, Jr., "Woodlawn Begins to Flex Its Muscles," *Presbyterian Life*, September 15, 1962, pp. 12-15, 41-42; Stephen C. Rose, "Saul Alinsky and His Critics," *Christianity and Crisis*, July 20, 1964, pp. 143-52; "Negative Votes on Alinsky," *Christianity and Crisis*, December 28, 1964, pp. 266-67; Walter Kloetzli, *The Church and the Urban Challenge* (Philadelphia: Fortress Press, 1961), pp. 47-65; Elinor Richey, "The Slum That Saved Itself," *The Progressive*, October, 1963, pp. 26-29; Charles E. Silberman, "Up from Apathy—The Woodlawn Experiment," *Commentary*, May, 1964, pp. 51-58; "Woodlawn Controversy," *Commentary*, October, 1964, pp. 14-22.

[4] Reported in the *Chicago Sun-Times*, April 12, 1961, p. 3.

The early goals of TWO appeared to some to be an attempt to block the University of Chicago in its plans to expand its campus in the area south of the Midway. Others saw TWO as an antiurban renewal organization. Still others felt it was an effort to restrict the movement of Negroes into all-white neighborhoods on Chicago's south side. Some of the leaders of TWO contended it represented a means of changing the status quo, while others saw it as a means of preserving the status quo (halt the expansion of the University of Chicago, stop urban renewal, and slow the Negro movement into white neighborhoods).

Certainly a basic motive in the creation of TWO was the acquisition of power. It was expected that this power would enable the people of Woodlawn to obtain a seat at the bargaining table and to influence the decisions of city and university leaders.

One of the earliest targets of TWO was the merchants in the area who were accused of cheating their customers. Next came attacks on the slum landlords, the city's urban renewal program, the University of Chicago, and the Chicago Board of Education. It conducted a very effective voter registration campaign and also engaged its own planning consultant in an effort to offer a counter proposal to the renewal plans of the city and the university.

More recently the IAF helped to organize the Northwest Community Organization (NCO) in a predominantly all-white heavily Roman Catholic section of Chicago about three miles northwest of the Loop. This has been a much less spectacular effort than TWO, and thus far the emphasis appears to have been on conservation, leadership development, and vigorous opposition to urban renewal. This effort began in 1961 when twenty-two Roman Catholic priests met with Alinsky to secure his advice and help. Eventually the Roman Catholic churches raised the $54,000 necessary for launching this venture. Three years after the first

95

organizational meeting was held, critics of NCO were charging that it had been "taken over" by local political leaders.

In each of these three communities a number of clergymen became sufficiently concerned over the deterioration of their neighborhood and the apparent inability of the residents to control their own destiny that they felt constrained to take action. In each case clergymen first began discussing the problem among themselves and eventually concluded that they lacked the expertize necessary for solving the problems. In each case they invited Alinsky in to discuss alternative courses of action and concluded that if the community were organized the people would gain the power to work out solutions to their problems.

These three organizations plus the Back of the Yards Council, are the four "effective" efforts at community organization referred to in the opening paragraph of this chapter. These four organizations also illustrate the methods and techniques espoused by Saul Alinsky and the Industrial Areas Foundation.[5]

First of all, he does not go into any community unless invited by leaders from the community. In the three most recent episodes in Chicago, as well as in recent discussions in other cities, the group extending this invitation was composed largely of clergy-

[5] For a more comprehensive statement see Alinsky, *Reveille for Radicals;* Silberman, *Crisis in Black and White,* p. 327; Nicholas von Hoffman, "Reorganization in the Casbah," *Social Progress,* April, 1962, pp. 33-44; Alinsky, "Citizen Participation and Community Organization in Planning and Urban Renewal," a pamphlet published by IAF and consisting of a paper presented by Alinsky on January 29, 1962. An extraordinarily revealing self-portrait of Alinsky is in Marion K. Sanders, "The Professional Radical: Conversations with Saul Alinky," *Harper's Magazine,* June, 1965, pp. 37-47, and "A Professional Radical Moves In on Rochester," *Harper's Magazine,* July, 1965, pp. 52-59. For two other descriptions of Alinsky's methods see Thomas D. Sherrard and Richard C. Murray, "The Church and Neighborhood Community Organization," *Social Work,* July, 1965, pp. 3-14; " 'Radical' Teaches Revolt to Clerics," *New York Times,* August 2, 1965, p. 33. See also Gibson Winter, "The Churches and Community Organization," *Christianity and Crisis,* May 31, 1965, pp. 119-22.

men. The persons doing the inviting are expected to secure the necessary funds to finance the operation.

Second, organizers employed by the IAF come into the community to (1) "plot the power pattern," (2) "search out and evaluate the local leaders," (3) gather statistics and other data on the community, (4) discover the grievances of the residents, (5) bring people together so they can articulate their frustrations and problems, and (6) solicit suggestions on solutions and methods of achieving solutions. It is during this stage that the organizers "rub raw the sores of discontent."

Third, a demonstration of the value of power is provided. Instead of talking about the theory or the benefits of organization, a direct action approach is utilized. In Woodlawn the public and widely publicized attacks on merchants who allegedly cheated their customers provided an example of direct action and the use of power. It could be a rent strike, a march on city hall, or picketing a slum landlord living in a wealthy suburb. In each the target for the attack has to be personified and direct action taken against this "enemy of the people." The demonstration must be related to the expressed grievances of the people; it must be a simple, easily understood problem; it should be one which can produce immediate results; above all else, it must illustrate the *power of organization*.

The next step usually is to create a temporary neighborhood council which is replaced as soon as possible by a permanent organization. This council is made up of neighborhood organizations which select their own delegates to the council.

While this is going on, the IAF organizers are recruiting and training indigenous leaders to take over the leadership responsibilities. It is expected that the new neighborhood council will raise the funds necessary to carry on the effort and to provide for a paid staff.

A cardinal tenet of Alinsky's is that he and his staff will pull out of the community and turn the responsibility and authority over to "indigenous leadership" as soon as possible. He firmly believes that both the leadership and the financial support must be provided by the community, not by "outsiders."

Any analysis of Alinsky's methodology reveals a close resemblance to the procedures and techniques developed by organized labor. The labor union, however, sought to win concessions from a single firm or industry. Alinsky's efforts are directed toward winning concessions from the total community. This distinction must be borne in mind in evaluating both the use and the effectiveness of his methods.

In Chicago and other cities clergymen have had a major role in developing the local organization which issues the invitation, in raising the money necessary for bringing in the IAF, and in filling continuing leadership positions.

The Chicago experiences of Alinsky not only illustrate how he operates, they also provide the foundation on which both the supporters and the opponents of Alinsky and the IAF base their cases. Does Alinsky have the only answer to the problem of community organization? Or is he advocating techniques and methods that cannot be used by the Christian?

One way for the outsider to answer these and similar questions is to examine the claims of the supporters and the objections of the critics against a backdrop of the activities and accomplishments of Alinsky and the community councils which he and his staff have helped organize. Before doing that, however, it is necessary to make three observations.

First of all, few people today seriously contend that the Back of the Yards organization should be included in the evaluation. It is a unique case and does not offer a fair test of Alinsky's method. One veteran Chicago observer called it a "feudal fief," and the experience there has little relevance to reality in contemporary urban America.

Second, no responsible person can deny that in Chicago there are many very effective efforts in community organization of the health and social welfare variety. These agencies are in operation, and they are providing necessary services without a lot of fanfare but with a high degree of effectiveness. The controversy in Chicago, however, has largely excluded or overlooked this dimension of the community organization process.

Third, there *are* several other effective community organizations in Chicago which also are concerned with helping the people to help themselves but are not patterned on the IAF model. The Lincoln Park Conservation Association is an outstanding example of such an organization. There are others.

## The Pro-Alinsky Position

Perhaps the most impressive argument made by the supporters of the IAF and Alinsky is that his method of operation does help the dispossessed and the deprived acquire a sense of dignity and self-respect. They are able to accept the assistance and help they need with a new attitude. The conventional methods of delivering specialized health and welfare services have often built up in the recipient a sense of resentment. At times this appears to have been deliberate. The supporters of Alinsky contend that in Woodlawn and other areas the development of an autonomous community organization has enabled the residents of the community to retain or develop a sense of self, of dignity, and of self-respect. These advocates of the IAF method claim that it works, it does help the people become participants rather than recipients, and that that difference is crucial.

The development of new indigenous leaders in Woodlawn is often cited as another sign of the effectiveness of this approach.

An almost universal goal of community organization (at least as the term is used in this book) is the recruitment and training of indigenous leaders. These have emerged in Woodlawn—although it is also true that much of the top leadership has come from nonresidents and that other leaders previously held positions of leadership, all the new organization did was to redirect the focus of their activities.

While there is a major controversy in Chicago over the "power" of these four community organizations, most observers appear to agree the effort definitely has given the people in these neighborhoods a *louder* voice in the community decision-making process. Whether it is a more influential voice is unclear. Perhaps, as one pro-IAF churchman pointed out, "In our society the louder the voice, the more influential the speaker." Some students of the decision-making process would disagree with this analysis.

Even Alinsky's critics admit that one of his accomplishments in Chicago has been to demonstrate the value of an effective public relations operation in community organization. This is especially important in a large metropolis. There appears to be little question but that part of the strength of TWO, and to a far lesser degree of OSC and NCO, has been a result of an extraordinarily effective publicity campaign. Publicity is an extremely useful device for stimulating participation and overcoming apathy. It also helps develop within both the leaders and the followers a sense of importance and self-esteem. TWO has demonstrated that this need not be a flash-in-the pan effort, but that it can be sustained over a long period of time.

One of the major claims made by supporters of Alinsky is that his efforts produce democratic organizations. In the strictest sense of the word the proper term is "representative democracy," since the various constituent organizations choose their own delegates, and the annual meeting (often called "Congress") is quite unlike the New England town meeting. It is important to note that a small elite makes the decisions between the meetings of the larger delegated body. Policy decisions are made by this large group of delegates, but again the question keeps being raised: How democratic can an afternoon meeting be with 700 to 1,000 participants?

A frequent claim made by supporters of TWO is that the residents of Woodlawn did acquire power which they had not possessed previously. This is true. The extent of this power is another question, however. They gained the power of a *temporary veto* over the urban renewal program of the city and the expansion plans of the university. (The exercise of this veto power coincided with the defeat of a city bond issue for financing urban renewal which had the effect of a city-wide "veto" on urban renewal programs in Chicago. Which was the more influential veto is a debatable question.) This was only a temporary veto, however, for the renewal plans being put into effect in early 1965 bore a strong resemblance to the plans prepared several years earlier. Likewise the University of Chicago has proceeded with its expansion plans.

More recently the efforts of TWO have shifted to civil rights and education, and there is good reason to believe that the organization not only is making a witness but also is influencing attitudes and decisions. In both of these areas TWO has benefited from the national climate of opinion which has encouraged the civil rights movement and the efforts to improve the quality of education in the slums.

In late 1964 TWO contracted with the United States Department of Labor for a retraining program for unemployed residents of the area. (This is another example of how TWO has turned from a posture of conflict with existing structures of society to one of cooperation. The same pattern can be seen in the support given by TWO to the development of middle income housing in Woodlawn.)

It also should be noted that OSC, TWO, and NCO have been able to force the Democratic political machine and other institutions to take notice of these new forces in the change process. How much they have influenced these existing institutions is a hotly disputed question, however, and cannot be answered objectively.

One of the more persuasive arguments used on behalf of Alinsky has been that his methods do get things moving. When the IAF enters into a contract with a local group, this is followed by highly visible activity. Staff members come in. They survey the area. They talk to people. They listen. This is followed by a dramatic use of direct action. Interest is stimulated. Inertia and apathy are overcome. A local council is organized. All of this activity stands in sharp contrast to the years of dull meetings which preceded the invitation to Alinsky. As soon as feasible, Alinsky and his staff leave, turning the responsibility over to local leadership and perhaps maintaining a consultative relationship to the new council.

This pattern has encouraged churchmen in several northern cities invite Alinsky in and to contract with the IAF for help in organizing the residents of a community in their city.[6] A surprisingly large number of these churchmen have expressed reservations about the methodology of the IAF, but frequently have

---

[6] The entrance of the IAF into cities such as Rochester, Buffalo, Syracuse, and Kansas City has created considerable furor. Two excellent descriptive articles on what happened in one such city are, Jerrold K. Footlick, "Northern Cities Face a Negro Drive for Power," *National Observer*, May 10, 1965, and Erwin Knoll and Jules Witcover, "Fighting Poverty—and City Hall," *The Reporter*, June 3, 1965, pp. 19-22. See also Stephen C. Rose, "Rochester's Racial Rubicon," *Christianity and Crisis*, March 22, 1965, pp. 55-59, and James Ridgeway, "Saul Alinsky in Smugtown," *New Republic*, June 26, 1965, pp. 15-17; Jules Witcover, "Rochester Braces for Another July," *The Reporter*, July 15, 1965, pp. 33-35.

added, "I am not one hundred per cent happy with the IAF, and I hope someone will develop techniques more compatible with my value system. In the meantime I see no alternative but to go along with Alinsky. There seems to be no other effective method."

This is a rather unsophisticated attitude and suggests that the speaker may be unaware of other approaches to community organization, many of which were in use long before Alinsky began his recent efforts in Chicago.

In commenting on this situation one observer offered two comments. "First of all, I believe this response by many ministers overlooks a serious question. Is the highly visible activity of the IAF worth the cost, in dollars and in the polarization of the community? Second, I sometimes believe that Alinsky's biggest asset is the way he handles his publicity and public relations. He seems to have a sales pitch which is especially attractive to clergymen!"

## The Anti-Alinsky Position

The criticisms of those who oppose the methods and techniques of Saul Alinsky and the IAF not only raise important ethical questions, they also illustrate some of the central issues in community organization.

Inasmuch as most efforts to organize the poor and the powerless do involve Negroes, perhaps the criticisms by Negroes of Alinsky should be summarized first.

Negro critics of Alinsky contend that the only effective way a Negro community can organize is from within and with Negro leadership. Any community organization effort which brings in outsiders to organize the Negroes, they contend, is but another paternalistic move to manipulate the Negro. Furthermore, the new organization must have Negro leaders. They point to Wood-lawn, which was organized by IAF staff who were outsiders, and to TWO which includes both Caucasians and nonresidents among the top leaders, and insist that by definition such an organization is not indigenous.

These Negro critics add that when Caucasian residents and nonresidents invite nonresident Caucasians in to organize a Negro community, they are saying by their actions, "You Negroes are inferior and are incapable of organizing yourselves." In addition to being insulting, they argue, this is untrue, and they point to the hundreds of Negro churches, lodges, and clubs which are evidence of the Negro's ability to provide his own organizations.

The second criticism offered by Negroes of Alinsky is that he is a segregationist. They ignore his proclamations for racial justice in his book *Reveille for Radicals* and point instead to the Back of the Yards which has remained all-white while Negroes moved into nearby neighborhoods. They point to his testimony before the United States Commission on Civil Rights in May, 1959, to interviews and to writings in which he has supported a quota system which would permit Negroes to move into an area until they constituted 5 to 7 per cent of the population.[7]

Alinsky has suggested that a quota system be used which would "invite" into white neighborhoods a number of Negro families who would be screened to assure that the Negro newcomers would resemble the white residents in background and other characteristics. A powerful community organization would handle the screening and invitation process and would maintain the percentage of Negro residents at the desired level by controlling the sale of property.

With this understanding of Alinsky's view of the structure and

[7] The most accessible statement of this position of Alinsky can be found in his article, "The Urban Immigrant," in Thomas T. McAvoy, ed., *Roman Catholicism and the American Way of Life* (Notre Dame, Ind.; University of Notre Dame Press, 1959), pp. 142-55.

purpose of community organization, it is rather easy to understand why some Negroes are critical of Alinsky and of any neighborhood council created by the IAF.

In all fairness it must be added that Alinsky also has stated on numerous occasions that he is opposed to the use of his methods to perpetuate segregation. Furthermore, while in their early days both OSC and TWO were charged with being devices to prevent the movement of Negroes into white neighborhoods, since the withdrawal of the IAF both have become strong supporters of the civil rights movement.

The most widespread criticisms of Alinsky and his methods have been focused not on the race issue, but rather on his methods. The critics contend that he lets the ends justify the means—a position which Alinsky openly admits to holding— that he advocates the acquisition of power for the sake of power, that he shows no reluctance to use power for destructive purposes, that his methods produce authoritarian rather than democratic organizations, and that none of his efforts in Chicago really have produced the indigenous leadership which is an expressed goal of all organizers.

On the power issue Alinsky does not quarrel with his critics. He openly advocates his central point that the only purpose of community organization is the redistribution of power. He contends that this is the only way to make democracy work. He admits that he has stirred up controversy for the sake of controversy. He admits that direct action is as useful for organizational purposes as it is for correcting a bad situation. He has stated that he is concerned with goals and that the end does justify the means. What other way, he asks, can you evaluate the means except by the end?

From another direction comes a very different criticism of Alinsky's position on power. These critics contend that Alinsky has underemphasized the political aspects of power and has failed to recognize the possibilities of influencing social change through the influence of partisan political pressures. The argument is made that government is the greatest single force in our society, and therefore anyone seeking to affect the course of events should seek to gain a controlling or influential voice in government rather than to depend on a direct confrontation.

For several years Harold Fey, former editor of *The Christian Century,* and others have accused Alinsky of using Marxist tactics of class warfare.[8] The words of Alinsky and Von Hoffman (who was the chief organizer in Woodlawn but later left IAF to become a reporter for the *Chicago Daily News*) lend support to the charges of Fey and others. Both Alinsky and Von Hoffman have contended that a community must be "disorganized" before it can be organized on the new model. In practice IAF organizers have used the threat, "Join us or be destroyed." In practice they have sought to destroy or neutralize existing community organizations in order to establish their agency as the dominant organization in the community. This tactic reminds one more of the teachings of Lenin and Mao Tse-tung than of Marx, but even in Woodlawn it has been far from completely effective in removing internal dissent.

Critics of Alinsky assert that there is an unnecessary amount of villification of the "enemy" and that the resulting polarization of the community inhibits the dynamics of the problem-solving process.

In both theory and practice Alinsky has urged the use of the

[8] For an elaboration of this argument see the following articles and editorials in *The Christian Century:* Everett C. Parker, "How Chelsea Was Torn Apart," February 3, 1960, pp. 130-33; "Open or Closed Cities?" May 10, 1961, pp. 579-80; "Revolution—What Kind?" July 18, 1962, pp. 879-81; "Exploiting Urban Decay," February 12, 1964, pp. 195-97; "The Greatest Good for All," June 30, 1965, pp. 827-28.

"devil theory" of organization. This method involves the selection of a scapegoat as the cause of the community's problem and then the launching of an attack on that scapegoat. For example, in Woodlawn the first devil to be attacked was the merchant who cheated his customers. Later the University of Chicago was identified as the enemy. In the NCO the enemy was the city administration in general and one political leader in particular.

In each case the identification and attack on the enemy causes people to band together in support of a united front. The excitement of the battle, the hope of victory, and the thrill of participating in a righteous cause all have proved to be effective organizational tools. Whether this be class warfare or merely a gimmick for organizing a community is a question which sharply divides Alinsky's supporters from his critics. (It is impossible to find any basis other than the very limited similarity in tactics to support the allegation of "Marxism." Furthermore, no credible evidence has been produced to substantiate the charges of "Communism" which have been leveled at Alinsky and the IAF.)

Perhaps the most effective response to the class warfare charge, and also the most devastating criticism of the IAF techniques is that in many respects it resembles a middle-class effort.[9] This is a somewhat difficult argument to follow, for much of the IAF rhetoric is based on the assumptions that (1) there is a proletariat, (2) alienation is increasing, (3) the ruling elite can and must be disposed of, (4) persons at the bottom of the social heap can and must be given the opportunity for leadership, and (5) the status quo must be altered sharply and rapidly.

[9] The idea that the IAF approach is basically a middle-class movement is not original with the author. A more extensive statement of this point was made in a speech by Robert C. Hoover, "Community Organization or the Revolution of the Everyday" delivered on May 8, 1963 to the annual meeting of the Garden Valley Neighborhood House in Cleveland, Ohio.

In Chicago, however, the IAF-sponsored "revolution" appears to be a middle-class effort. A large proportion of the funds necessary for the effort have come from middle- and upper-class sources. Most of the leaders are clearly drawn from the middle and upper classes of society and the "indigenous" leadership has been drawn largely from the middle class rather than the lower class. (One third of the families in Woodlawn had a family income of $6,000 or more in 1963.) A new ruling elite has emerged, alienation continues to be a problem rather than a source of strength, much of the early effort was spent to preserve the status quo, and many of the new goals have a strong middle-class ring. In 1964, after he had left the IAF, Von Hoffman estimated that no more than 2 percent of the residents of Woodlawn had been involved in TWO. The high membership dues levied by TWO made it difficult for the poor to be adequately represented.

While supporters of the IAF approach strongly object to such allegations, Hoover may have been right when he said, "von Hoffman is a bourgeois revolutionist." The idea of political revolution is a middle-class concept.[10] The leaders of the American Revolution were members of the middle class as were those who invited the IAF into the southwest community, into Woodlawn, and into the northwest area of Chicago. It is difficult to think of a neighborhood council president with seven years of education beyond high school as a member of the lower class. It is difficult to think of housing renting for $100 a month or selling for $15,000 as lower-class housing.

When the question of human resource development comes up, the supporters of the IAF contend that its methods do produce personal growth in the individuals involved in the neighborhood

[10] For an elaboration of this point see Erich Fromm, *The Sane Society* (New York: Holt, Rinehart & Winston, 1955), pp. 260-69.

council, and that it is the most effective channel of adult educa-tion they have encountered. The critics argue that the organiza-tions founded by IAF have been issue-centered rather than person-centered and have failed to alter the lives or the outlook of the masses. This argument can be settled only by an extensive research project and it is far too early to predict the results—but this will be a crucial item in the final evaluation of IAF.

The critics also argue that the supporters of IAF have been overly generous in crediting the community organizations with achievements which cannot be substantiated. For example, three of the victories claimed for TWO are that it eliminated double shifts in the Woodlawn schools, forced the city to agree that new housing would be provided in Woodlawn *before* demolition be-gan, and caused the city and the university to alter their renewal and expansion plans. The critics respond that the board of edu-cation had planned new schools to eliminate half-day classes before TWO was organized and that half-day classes were elimi-nated all over the city, not just in Woodlawn; that the city had always planned to provide new relocation housing before demolition began; and that the plans of the city and university have been delayed but not altered.

Some of Alinsky's friends, as well as his critics, assert that while the IAF staff is active during the survey and initial organizing efforts, Alinsky pulls out of these situations prematurely. This tends to result, contend the critics, in an overemphasis on highly visible, but minor issues. It also means that the less visible, but more fundamental long-term problems are neglected. In some communities, it has been alleged that Alinsky withdrew before the new organization was able to stand on its own feet—while it still needed the continuing guidance of the consultant.

On the other hand, this requirement by Alinsky and the IAF

that he and his staff do withdraw as soon as possible should encourage the early development of indigenous leadership. It also is an effective answer to the charge that he is trying to build a super organization composed of several "controlled" neighborhood councils which together would form the basis for a new political group or party.

One of the reasons that it is difficult to evaluate the work of Alinsky is that he has failed to provide objective responses to the criticisms leveled at him. This has distressed some of his supporters as much or more than it has his opponents. When pressed for a response he tends to denounce the critics and their goals rather than to respond to their criticisms.

## An Attempt at an Evaluation

This communications gap between Alinsky and his critics makes it impossible to present an adequate summary of the two positions since there is no argreement on the issues, much less on the facts. Nevertheless, the importance of this controversy, and the recent moves by IAF staff members into Detroit, Los Angeles, Kansas City, Syracuse, Rochester, Buffalo, and other cities makes it necessary to attempt a brief evaluation of this controversial venture in community organization.

Out of this investigation come these five generalizations. Admittedly they do not tell the whole story, but they are offered in an effort to simplify a very complex controversy.

1. The basic dividing line between the supporters of Alinsky and his critics is theological. The theological point of view of the individual determines his value system, and the difference in value systems is what separates Alinsky from his critics. This can be illustrated most clearly by the debate over the question of whether the end justifies the means. The supporters of Alinsky

appear to be able to dismiss this as a minor issue. The critics regard it as a fundamental question.

2. This difference in value systems is reflected in the relative concern expressed over the methods employed by the staff of the IAF. The critics argue strenuously that it is unchristian to suppress the right of dissent in a community, to "force" reluctant institutions to join the new neighborhood council, to use conflict for destructive purposes, to polarize a community and thus increase the degree of alienation, to play on the fears and hostilities of individuals in order to win their allegiance, to create controversy for the sake of controversy, and to seek power as an end rather than as a means.

The supporters respond that most of these issues are of secondary importance. The primary goals are social justice and helping the destitute to regain the right of self-determination and the powerless to achieve a place of power in the community decision-making process.

The way this difference in value systems divides Alinsky's supporters from his opponents is vividly illustrated by an exchange between two old friends who met and found they were on opposite sides in this controversy. Near the end of the conversation the one who was an ardent supporter of the methodology developed and used by Alinsky said, "Friend, I think I finally understand why you are so strongly opposed to Alinsky. You honestly believe that lying, cheating, duplicity, and attacking innocent people are wrong. In the world where I live you can't really swing unless you're willing to let the end determine the means. Lying, cheating, duplicity, and villification are tools we use to get the job done in my world. However, if you really believe in the ethical code you proclaim, you have no choice but to go on attacking Alinsky and his techniques."

3. Two clear-cut lessons, which are acknowledged by most

observers, appear to have emerged from the Chicago experience.

(a) A community organization with a narrow focus such as those created by IAF cannot supply all the answers for a severely blighted community filled with the disadvantaged, the dispossessed, and the disfranchised. The broad array of health and welfare services which historically have been provided by public and conventional private agencies are still needed. Community organization *a la* Alinsky will not eliminate that need. In Chicago, as everywhere else, the leaders of the new community organizations eventually have found it necessary to work through the established structures and institutions of society rather than against them.

(b) The Chicago experience clearly demonstrates the value of money and staff. The OSC, TWO, and NCO have benefited from a large input of outside money and manpower. This, more than the methodology, probably has been responsible for the achievements of these three organizations. This, more than any other single factor, distinguishes them from other efforts in community organization in Chicago. Out of this experience has come what now appears to be the central question in community organization. How can the necessary funds be supplied without jeopardizing the autonomy of the organization?

4. Despite the barrage of publicity and the protestations, the argument that the Alinsky methods banish the apathy and the indifference of the lower classes remains to be proved. Woodlawn is cited as the dramatic illustration of effective organization of the lower classes; however, Woodlawn had been the scene of a vast quantity of organizational activity for years before TWO was formed. Woodlawn was a fertile ground for the IAF. True, there was apathy and despair and poverty in Woodlawn, but also present were a variety of organizations, a reservoir of experienced leaders, and a large number of middle-class persons. TWO

has drawn heavily from this reservoir of middle-class institutions, middle-class leadership, and from outside middle-class money. This is not intended to be a criticism of TWO, but it does demonstrate how difficult it is to reach the lower classes and how tempting it can be to use middle-class resources in a movement to "organize the masses of society." Furthermore, it should be noted that in Woodlawn the IAF did not have to compete with the powerful Democratic political machine which dominates many Chicago neighborhoods.

5. While the work and the techniques of Saul Alinsky in Chicago have aroused a tremendous controversy within Protestantism, and that controversy is now spreading to several other cities as religious groups elsewhere enlist the aid of the IAF, neither the man nor his organization appears to be taken seriously by politicians, political scientists, planners, social workers, social scientists, and others who are concerned about the city and its problems. One official in the human relations field commented rather cynically on the role of the clergy in supporting the IAF by saying, "Then there are the religious romantics who keep seeing the second coming of Christ in every guy who raises an indigenous protest movement." [11] Were it not for the interest of Protestant churchmen and the public relations skill of Alinsky, the man and his methods might already have disappeared from public view. It is not irrelevant to note that many of the persons responsible for inviting Alinsky and the IAF into urban centers in Kansas, Michigan, and New York have been active churchmen. Conspicuous by their absence have been the experienced politicians, the professional planners, the seasoned social workers, and professors of political science.

Perhaps there is both wisdom and relevance in the comment

[11] Quoted in *The Detroit News*, February 28, 1965, p. 16A.

of a social scientist who said, "You churchmen are the ones who have created this big controversy over Alinsky and his methods. Alinsky was just another honest, middle-class businessman who was going about the country selling his wares until some clergymen became interested in his product. Since then you churchmen have turned him into a national figure."

Regardless of the accuracy of this appraisal, no one can dispute the significance of the Chicago controversy in stimulating the churches' interest in community organization.[12]

In addition the controversy in Chicago has also caused churchmen to reexamine their ideas about power and the use of power in effecting social change.

[12] For a pro and con evaluation of the IAF, published after this chapter was written, see Philip M. Hauser, "Industrial Areas Foundation: A Criticism" and Douglas Still, "Industrial Areas Foundation: A Defense," *The Church and Community Organization*, ed. John R. Fry (New York: National Council of Churches, 1965), pp. 67-87.

Chapter Six
_____

# Problems of Power

The controversy in Chicago over community organization in general, and specifically over the methods of Saul Alinsky and the involvement of the churches, has generated widespread interest in the subject of power. Chicago was the first city in the nation to witness the widespread application of the theory that the acquisition and redistribution of power is the crucial element in the community organization process. This concept has spread to several other cities where the churches have begun to take an active role in community organization and this has aroused a major controversy within Protestantism over the emphasis on power.

The supporters of the churches' participation generally contend that their emphasis on power not only is morally right, it also is the only realistic approach to community organization. At the other extreme are the critics who argue that this dependence on power is nothing but a Leninist tactic of class warfare, and, whether it is practiced by churchmen or communities, it cannot be condoned by Christians. Others insist this reliance on power is most inappropriate for men who claim membership in a religious body founded on an ethic of love. Some churchmen find the entire subject of power distasteful and wish that the church would avoid any involvement in the use of power.

Actually much of the discussion over power, especially by those who find it an unpleasant or abhorrent subject, is either naive or irrelevant. All of life is an expression of power. Power pervades all relationships among persons and institutions. Power is simply the ability to influence the actions and decisions of others. The possession of power in social relationships is the capacity to compel other persons to act in a desired manner through the use of sanctions.

The parent holds power over the child. He can compel the child to go to bed, to attend school, or to "be good." He may do this through force, through the granting or withholding of approval, or through some other sanction. The child possesses power over the parent, and through the use of sanctions such as tears or smiles he often compels the parent to behave in the desired manner.

Power pervades relationships within the church. The pastor who wants or feels he needs the approval of his lay leader is subject to the power of that lay leader. The layman who wants or feels he needs the approval of his pastor is subject to the power of his pastor. In both cases the granting or withholding of approval is a sanction. In some denominations the congregation has the authority to hire and fire their minister. The possession of this sanction of dismissal may or may not give the congregation considerable power over the pastor; this will depend on how badly the minister wants to hold his job. In the Roman Catholic Church the sanction of excommunication gives the church great power over its members—or at least those members who do not want to face the consequences of excommunication.

There are many, many facets to this subject of power, and power has long been a topic of great interest to churchmen from Moses to Amos to Luther to Rauschenbusch to today's seminarian. The subject is far too extensive and complex to permit an adequate summary here; however, it is appropriate to offer several brief observations on power which are relevant to the process of community organization. These do not begin to exhaust the subject, but they may be helpful to the churchman who is concerned about the role of power in community organization.[1]

1. *An important distinction exists between power and authority.* Power which is formally recognized in the value system of the social structure is referred to as authority. This would include the authority of a father, a mayor, a president of a corporation, a foreman, or a bishop. Those to whom this power has been delegated are referred to as persons with authority or "authority is thus the expected and legitimate possession of power."[2] The others who have the capacity to apply sanctions and to influence the decision-making process, but have not been formally vested with the authority for the use of that influence, are referred to simply as holders of power. Thus a clash between the mayor and the representative of a neighborhood association which has gathered enough influence to block an urban renewal program that has received the formal approval of the city government is a conflict between authority (legitimate power) and informal power.

[1] For an extremely readable and provocative discussion of power see Robert M. MacIver, *Power Transformed* (New York: The Macmillan Company, 1964) especially pp. 75-218. For another point of view on the place of power in American society see Sylvia K. Selekman and Benjamin M. Selekman, *Power and Morality in a Business Society* (New York: McGraw-Hill Book Company, 1956).

[2] Harold D. Lasswell and Abraham Kaplan, *Power and Society* (New Haven: Yale University Press, 1950), p. 133.

2. *There often is a distinction between power and leadership.* The holder of power may be able to compel others to follow him. The word "leader" infers a voluntary relationship. In the early history of community organization the tendency was to seek out the major holders of community power and to enlist them to be the leaders. Apparently it was assumed that leaders of this stature would secure a following rather easily and be very effective. In recent years the practice has changed and the emphasis is to recruit and train indigenous leaders who are not holders of power, but who may have the capacity to enlist voluntary followers. Thus the focus has shifted from an effort to organize around existing power figures to an effort to redistribute power by introducing new leaders into the decision-making process.

A basic assumption of the community organization process is that leadership ability is not an inborn quality but that leaders can be trained. Experience has proved this to be possible. Preparing a man to be a leader is one means of helping that man acquire power. This is one means by which community organization can result in the redistribution of power.

3. *The exercise of power is determined by values and relationships.* The possession of power can be identified by the capacity to coerce, but coercion is dependent upon a value system. This power to coerce exists only within a system of relationships and values. As values change or relationships are altered, the capacity to coerce may change, and this will result in a fluctuation in power. Voters hold power over elected officials because the elected official usually seeks the approval of the voters. This relationship is built into our political system, and voter approval is necessary for an elected official to remain in office. This approval is valued most highly during the months immediately preceding an election. When an elected official decides not to be a candidate again, the power of the voters over this official declines sharply. In this

changed relationship and changed value system a neighborhood association may lose much of its power over the local alderman. However, if the alderman still places a high value on peace and harmony in his ward, he is vulnerable to coercion through picketing and other direct action efforts.

In a similar manner persons who are displeased with a community organization effort may attempt to stop it by the exercise of their power. This means they must first discover what is valued by the local leadership and then seek to impose sanctions through the appropriate relationship. The best illustration of this has been the economic coercion applied against Negroes. White power figures who opposed a course of action being considered by the Negro community often could stop it by economic pressures against the Negro leaders. This might be the threatened loss of employment, termination of credit, or foreclosure on loans. Historically, the one Negro leader immune to such threats of economic reprisal was the Negro clergyman. He may have held the same economic values as his parishioners, but his economic relationship was to the Negro community and not to the white community. More recently other Negro leaders have come largely from the ranks of Negro professionals—doctors, dentists, lawyers, clergymen, and professional civil rights leaders who do not have a relationship to the white community which makes them vulnerable to economic reprisals.

4. *The concept of a single community power structure is a myth.* Much of the talk by churchmen in community organization has been about "the power structure" and opposition to this power structure has been a prime motivation in many community organization efforts. This is an extremely oversimplified explanation of how power is structured. In every community there are many power *centers,* and the coalitions of power groups which constitute a single power center are constantly shifting.

These coalitions will vary as the issues vary. Occasionally at a certain point in history one power center appears to dominate the landscape of power. This may have been the case in Atlanta in the 1950's or in Dallas in the 1960's, but basically the idea of a single monolithic power structure is a very poor representation of a far more dynamic reality.

Thus the person who turns to community organization as a means of combatting the tyranny of the power structure would be well advised to think instead in terms of many power centers. His efforts in community organization are but a means of creating a new power group. This new power group will then be looking for allies to form a new power center.[3]

5. *Power is necessary for anyone seeking to participate in the community decision-making process.* This affirmation is self-evident by definition. Power is the capacity to influence others and the decisions of others. Therefore anyone seeking to be an effective participant in the decision-making process must possess power. The more power he holds, the more influential he will be.

Despite the obvious nature of this statement, many churchmen naively expect to walk in, take a seat at the bargaining table, and influence the decisions made there. Perhaps they expect their "moral view" will win adherents. Perhaps they expect their "impartial and objective position" will influence others. Whatever the reason, this is one of the most common errors made by churchmen. In order to influence the decision-making process, a person *must* have power. This may be the power of specialized knowledge. It may be the power of a charismatic personality. It may be the power which is a part of delegated authority. The

[3] The best book on the community decision-making process is Robert A. Dahl, *Who Governs?* (New Haven: Yale University Press, 1961). For a clergyman's point of view see George D. Younger, *The Church and Urban Power Structure* (Philadelphia: The Westminster Press, 1963).

source of power may vary, but the fact of power must be recognized as crucial.

One of the goals of many leaders in community organization is to create a new power center, thus providing its spokesmen with power that will enable them to influence the decision-making process.[4]

6. *Authority can be granted or given, but power must be earned.* Occasionally one hears the statement, "All power must be taken, no one can give you power." This is true only if the distinction is maintained between power and authority. However, it must be remembered that authority includes power. The holder of authority possesses power, and authority can be given. The man who owns a million-dollar business can walk up to you and say, "I am appointing you manager of my firm and giving you full authority to take any action you wish." By so doing he gives you the power to fire the employees or to sell the business. You are given power, but you acquire this power only because it is an ingredient of the authority given to you. The father of a young prince dies and the son is *given* power, but only the power inherent in the authority which goes with being king. All power which he seeks beyond that which is implicit in his hereditary role must be earned.

On the other hand, power, as separate from authority, must be earned. It cannot be acquired by gift. Thus a neighborhood association has to earn whatever power it acquires. An individual has to earn his power to influence the community decision-making process.

The importance of this distinction in how power is acquired was illustrated by an incident in a midwestern city in 1964.

---

[4] The argument that the acquisition of power is the only way Negroes and other disadvantaged groups can solve their problems is the central thesis of Charles E. Silberman, *Crisis in Black and White*.

The official local antipoverty committee had been selected and many people, including several government officials in Washington, felt that it did not give adequate representation to the poor. Out of the many protests over the composition of the committee emerged the question, who has the power to speak for Protestantism on this and similar issues? Two answers were offered to this question.

In one the executive of the local council of churches circulated a memorandum describing the problem and suggested that the council of churches be given the power to represent Protestantism in the arena of community decision making. Subsequently at a meeting attended by six or seven denominational executives a motion was offered and duly approved that the council be given this power. The subsequent course of events demonstrated that this decision had no effect on the community decision-making process.

At about the same time a small group of Protestant churchmen, about one half of whom were clergymen, began to meet informally and later organized a citizens committee on the problems of poverty. The chairman was an energetic minister who had had considerable training and experience in social welfare. This group began a systematic protest against the exclusion of the poor from the local antipoverty committee which was dominated by white, middle-class suburbanites. They gained a measure of local support and eventually presented such an impressive case to the federal government that the Washington officials agreed to withhold further grants to that city until the local committee was reconstituted to be more representative. Through work and knowledge they had *earned* not only the capacity to exercise a measure of coercion on this immediate issue, but they also *earned* recognition as the Protestant spokesmen on the subject of poverty in general and also on several other issues. The power to be a party to the resolution of conflict must be earned; it cannot be given!

7. *There are many sources of power.* One of the overemphases in the current state of community organization is on the use of organization as a source of power and on conflict as a means of redistributing power. The community organization process is a source of power and in effect can create new power through human resource development and through organization.[5]

MacIver also contends in a very impressive argument that knowledge is the prime source of power and that it is rapidly outdistancing all other sources. He also points out that force is rapidly declining in importance as a source of power. For centuries force was the primary source of power on the world scene. This is no longer true. This may be the most important lesson history has to offer to the art of community organization. This emphasis on knowledge as the primary source of power is generally accepted by most students of human affairs, of business, and of international affairs, but not by many of the practitioners in community organization who tend to continue to stress the use of force.

Other sources include charisma, organization, possessions, convictions, the accident of birth, and conflict. Churchmen interested in community organization *primarily* as a source of power would do well to consider the various sources of power.

8. *The easiest power to acquire is the power of veto; the hardest power to acquire is the power to initiate and implement.* American society seeks a consensus. It operates most smoothly when it is functioning on the basis of a consensus. Most people prefer a consensus to a simple majority. This generalization

---

[5] For an extremely relevant discussion of organization as power see MacIver, *Power Transformed*, pp. 139-52.

applies to the church, to politics, to business, and to social agencies. The concept of rule by a consensus was best articulated by John C. Calhoun in his doctrine of concurrent majorities. Despite the repudiation of this position in the Civil War, the search for a consensus remains one of the primary functions of government.

The search for a consensus automatically vests power in the minority who can prevent the development of a consensus. It also means that it often requires a great deal more power to make a positive decision, since this may require the building of a consensus, than it does to prevent action.[6]

This distinction is of vital importance to the community organization which may acquire the power to veto a decision, but not realize that it is far from having sufficient power to secure approval and implementation of a counter proposal.

9. *The established holders of power generally prefer cooperation to conflict.* Conflict is threatening to the established holders of power. Conflict is disruptive. Conflict is one of the fastest means of redistributing power. Conflict means the game will be played by a new set of rules under new conditions. For these and similar reasons the established holders of both authority and power generally go to some length to avoid conflict. They much prefer to work through the process of cooperation because they are more familiar with the methods of cooperation and usually are the ones who make the rules by which the game of cooperation will be played.

This does not mean, however, that the established holders of power are afraid of conflict. Frequently they are willing to yield more to the *threat* of conflict than they would have to

[6] For a more extended statement of this argument see Lyle E. Schaller, "Majority Rule, Minority Veto, and the Search for a Consensus," *Mayor and Manager,* VII (April, 1964), 22-26.

yield if conflict should occur. This suggests that persons interested in the use of conflict to achieve social change might be well advised to maximize the *threat* of conflict and minimize the actual *use* of conflict.

10. *The extent of power generally is overestimated.* Both Dwight D. Eisenhower and John F. Kennedy remarked, after they had been elected to the nation's highest office, that the President of the United States actually has much less power than people attribute to the post.

People generally attribute to others more power than they possess. One man who was reputed to be the most powerful figure in his community was asked if it were true that he held a tremendous amount of power. He replied, "Yes, I guess I do, so long as I don't try to use it."

This point is often overlooked by those who seek to achieve great social changes by either persuading or coercing the powerful to make the decisions which will produce the changes. Usually the power to do this is far less than is attributed to the person. If this is not understood it can lead to unnecessary misunderstandings and fruitless conflict.

11. *The distinction between the overt use of power and the covert use of power is underemphasized.* John C. Bennett has stressed this distinction in speaking to persons interested in community organization. He points out that foot-dragging by the established holders of power in the face of demands for social change may be as coercive in fact as the demonstrations in the street.[7]

This argument frequently is used in an effort to convince congregations and individuals that by doing nothing they are

[7] This point is made in an extremely significant article by Bennett, "The Church and Power Conflicts," *Christianity and Crisis*, XXV (March 22, 1965), 47-51.

in fact exercising power in a covert manner to resist social change. It is a very persuasive argument and points up an important aspect of power which frequently is overlooked by critics of the use of conflict.

12. *The acquisition and possession of power frequently changes the holder.* This is a point which is easy to see in others, but difficult to see in oneself. Lord Acton said, "Power tends to corrupt . . ." and this is generally accepted to be true—about the other person.

13. *The concentration on the acquisition of power can thwart the human resource development aspect of community organization.* If during the community organization process the emphasis is placed on the acquisition of power—and this is always a very real possibility—there is a danger that the effort will leave the "followers" or members of the association little better off in terms of their own maturity or development than they were when the process began.

When power becomes the primary goal there is a temptation to utilize the best available leadership whether it is indigenous or imported—rather than to spend the time and effort to recruit and train new leaders. There is a tendency to postpone until later, "when there is more time," the unglamorous and slow process of helping people discover and define their own needs and select their own solutions.

The struggle for power is a complex battle and does require many of the skills which the organizer possesses and which the people with whom he is working have yet to acquire. In this situation it is easy for everyone to agree that the professional change agent should drop his "enabling" role and concentrate on the redistribution of power. All too often the desire to improve the means of achieving a goal becomes an end in itself and the original goal is forgotten.

These observations on power and the use of power are not intended to discourage churchmen from seeking and using power in a creative manner. Power is an integral part of the social scheme and is exercised by all churchmen every day. These observations are offered to help interested persons recognize some of the issues which do arise from the use of power in community organization.

These brief introductory comments on power also set the stage for posing the crucial question to the Christian who sees a conflict between the use of power and the ethic of love. He may feel constrained from participating in a community organization effort because it requires him to operate at a level below the Christian ideal of love in the use of power. What is the relationship between love and power? Between love and justice? Between power and justice?

## Love, Power, and Justice

Perhaps the crucial point from which to begin is the contention of John C. Bennett, Reinhold Niebuhr, H. Richard Niebuhr, and others that justice may be the highest attainable level of motivation for relationships among groups in a community. The motivation of love should govern all of the actions of the individual Christian, and it can be the controlling factor in his relationships with other individuals.[8]

When the relationships are more complex, as between groups, or between organizations, then the highest attainable level of motivation is justice. In this sinful world the constant threat is that the level of motivation will descend to one of selfish self-

[8] The serious student of this question will turn to Paul Tillich, *Love, Power and Justice* (New York: Oxford University Press, 1960). For other points of view see Richard B. Brandt, ed., *Social Justice* (Englewood Cliffs, N. J.: Prentice-Hall, 1962).

interest. This danger exists in all levels of relationships and in all combinations of relationships among individuals, groups, and organizations. As was pointed out in Chap. 2, by definition community organization is concerned primarily with the relationships on a more complex level than those involving only individuals or only groups of people. The community council will be relating to other organizations or similarly complex social structures, to groups, and perhaps to individuals. On these levels of complexity justice is the highest attainable level of motivation.

This effort to explain the relationship of power, love, and justice is based on two assumptions: (1) man is a sinner, and (2) unless power is sought and used for moral purposes it is almost certain to be a corrupting force, and it becomes impossible for the Christian to justify his efforts in seeking or using power. As Dan W. Dodson has pointed out, when power is used to uphold moral principles, it is very different from power being used to uphold or gain private privilege.[9]

The other aspect of this discussion which merits attention here is the use of the community organization process to acquire power and the goal of human resource development. These are not incompatible goals; however, there is always the danger that the attractiveness of power to sinful man will make the acquisition and use of power the primary goal. To the Christian, justice requires that the primary goal must always be human resource development. Often the acquisition of power is necessary to achieve this primary goal—however, the acquisition and use of power should never become the primary goal; it is always a means and never an end.

The community organization process requires the individual, as part of a complex social structure, to operate at a level below the

[9] "Power as a Dimension of Education," *The Journal of Educational Sociology,* XXXV, No. 5, 213.

Christian ideal, but this is not an adequate excuse for non-participation. Much of the injustice in the world is a result of the nonparticipation of persons who call themselves Christians. The exercise of power should not force the Christian into non-participation. Rather, power, and the tensions produced by the use of power, should increase the Christian's awareness that his role in the community organization process also calls for a ministry of reconciliation.

Chapter Seven

# The Ministry of Reconciliation

"For seven years I served as the pastor of an inner city church. During those seven years I did everything in my power to bridge the gulf between the residents of the inner city and the suburbs, I tried to be a reconciler, minimizing the differences of education, income, and housing, and stressing the similarities as persons and as children of God. I spent hundreds and hundreds of hours bringing people together from the different compartments of our urban society, trying to help them know one another as persons.

"Now with my new involvement in community organization I find myself trying to widen the gulf in order to dramatize the issues of poverty, segregation, and despair."

With these comments a pastor who left his pulpit to become a full-time community organizer for the home missions department of his denomination described the basic dilemma which confronts the Christian in this field. As he seeks to promote social justice he finds conflict and division to be two of his most valuable tools. On the other hand he has a natural Christian concern to reconcile the differences which divide men and to resist the hostility and alienation which pervade his world. He finds himself much more at ease trying to build a consensus than he does in recruiting a group of residents to march on a picket line.

What help is there for the Christian who finds himself in this dilemma? Is the spirit of reconciliation incompatible with the conflict theory of social change? What help and insights does Christian theology offer the community organizer?

Some churchmen will resolve this dilemma by contending that the pursuit of social justice is the supreme goal for Christians in intergroup relations. They contend that the task of effecting planned social change is basically a struggle among power blocs, that justice is the highest attainable goal in this situation, and that the end does justify the means.

Others will find these explanations totally inadequate and will continue to be troubled. They remember the words of Jesus in the Beatitudes and his commendation of the meek and of the peacemakers. They remember the injunction of Jesus to love one's enemies.[1] For them the experiences and reflections of churchmen who have been actively involved in community organizations may be helpful. The dilemma is not a new one and experience has provided several valuable insights.

The first of these is the importance of a sound theological base. If one thinks of the purpose of the church as the continuous reenactment of the Crucifixion, a firm base is provided for the ministry of reconciliation. The Christian has no alternative but to choose the way of reconciliation, which is also the way of self-giving, self-sacrificing, and suffering love. It is true that when

---

[1] For an extremely relevant elaboration of this point see Dietrich Bonhoeffer, *The Cost of Discipleship* (New York: The Macmillan Company, 1960), pp. 131-38.

Jesus drove the money changers out of the temple contemporary observers of the scene probably found it difficult to think of him as a reconciling force. It is also true, however, that the crucial New Testament image of Jesus is not as the person who used conflict to cleanse the temple, but rather as the Son of God who died on the cross.[2] The two events are not equal in significance. Jesus was primarily a reconciling agent witnessing to the love of God for his children. His followers must recognize and react to the centrality of the cross in Christianity.

In this spirit the churchman who marches on a picket line not only is witnessing to his concern for the oppressed, he also is suffering with those against whom he is protesting. He marches in a spirit of protest, but also in a spirit of reconciliation. He marches knowing that he is protesting the actions of a sinful man in a sinful world, but also knowing that he too is a sinner in need of God's forgiving and redemptive love.

Out of these and similar experiences has come dramatic proof that the Christian can resort to the use of nonviolent conflict without danger of this degenerating into violence, *if he acts in a spirit of reconciliation* which is based on a firm biblical foundation. Conflict and reconciliation are not incompatible.[3]

The second lesson from experience is illustrated by the statement of one clergyman who said, "I would never resort to the use of conflict against a man or his agency unless I were also able and willing to call on him and talk with him in a spirit of love and concern."

This comment illustrates two important considerations. First of all, there is the dimension of pastoral care. In community

---

[2] For a helpful discussion of the central importance of the cross and the concept of reconciliation see Emil Brunner, *The Mediator* (Philadelphia: The Westminster Press, 1947), pp. 435-54.

[3] For a brief, but helpful, look at these basic issues see Paul Ramsey, *Christian Ethics and the Sit-In* (New York: Association Press, 1961).

organization there is a great need for continuing face-to-face encounters between persons on different sides of an issue as well as between persons who share the same point of view. In these encounters there is the opportunity for expression of concern for the other person as a person. Our society is becoming increasingly depersonalized and these opportunities for face-to-face contacts are becoming more limited. When the Christian calls on the person who is his opponent on a social or economic issue, he may not be able to alter the other person's position, but he can always express a brotherly concern for that person who is also a child of God.

The other aspect of this face-to-face contact is that it may help to keep the personalities separate from the issues. When this is not done, there is a serious risk that the adverse emotional reaction to a man's position on this particular issue will be transferred to the man. There is a vast difference between hating the position held by a man and hating the man himself. The Christian is called to act in a spirit of love, mercy, and charity to both friend and foe, to both supporter and opponent, to both the oppressed and the oppressor.

Another dimension of this ministry of reconciliation is found within the congregation which becomes part of a community council. It is tempting for the pastor and a few laymen, who may see the need for action more clearly than most of the members, to move ahead rapidly. They can rationalize their aggressive leadership on the grounds that justice requires action *now*. The wise pastor, however, will recognize the necessity of bringing all the members along in this effort. Too often the active participation of a minister in community organization means that he has less time for pastoral calling. The ministry of reconciliation often requires him to *increase* the number of his pastoral calls as he assumes a more active role in the community. This may appear impossible simply because of the pressures of time. On the other hand, any other choice may mean that he has failed to fulfill his responsibility as a shepherd of his flock. Too often this has been the case and as the minister "got too far out in front" of his congregation, he found himself alienated from those whom he was trying to lead.

This responsibility for a redemptive ministry of reconciliation *within* the local church becomes clearer when presented within the context of organizational relationships. By definition community organization operates primarily at the level of organizations rather than at the level of person-to-person relationships (case work) or group relationships (group work). Within this framework it is too easy to think of the church as only another impersonal organization, rather than as a community of called-out believers. It is easy to think of the church as a single social unit, rather than as a dynamic community of individuals, many of whom may be threatened by any effort directed at planned social change. Within each organization participating in a community effort there is a need for this ministry of reconciliation.

A fourth area in the community organization process in which there is a need for this ministry of reconciliation is in minimizing unnecessary conflict for both the individual and the community. This is not to be construed as a denial of the necessity or validity of conflict, but not all conflict is necessary. As Martin Marty has pointed out, one function of religion is to serve as a buffer "in the face of diffuse and chaotic social change."[4]

Here there is a need for the redemptive and reconciling ministry of the church and of the individual Christian to help people accept and react creatively to change, rather than letting them

[4] "Epilogue: The Nature and Consequences of Social Conflict for Religious Groups," *Religion and Social Conflict*, p. 180.

134

be overwhelmed by the brutal force of conflict. At times this will require efforts to minimize both the extent and the consequences of conflict and efforts to reduce or prevent conflict which serves no creative purpose. At other times it means channeling conflict into new channels where it will be more creative and can be used to further positive goals.

Finally, there is a need for a pastoral ministry to those with whom the community council may be in conflict. Thus far this has been a badly neglected facet of the church's concern in the community organization process. Thus far the emphasis has been on having the church work with, and minister to, the poor, the oppressed, the dispossessed, and the powerless. This is a vital ministry, but it is not the only ministry the church is called to offer.

There is also a need for the church to provide a reconciling ministry to the affluent, the powerful, and those who benefit most from a preservation of the status quo. There are two aspects to this ministry. The first is the ministry to the person who becomes alienated from the world because he feels an ungrateful society does not appreciate his generosity and his contributions. Instead of receiving a letter of thanks for his financial or civic contributions, he looks out his window and sees pickets marching past his office building. This man needs assistance in comprehending the viewpoint of those whom he thinks he has been helping. He needs help in understanding why those he has helped respond in this manner.

The other aspect of this ministry of reconciliation is directed toward the individual who is not in a position of power, but who because of social, economic, racial, and geographical separation is unable to comprehend the aggressive attitude of those who seek rapid social change. He cannot understand why the Negro wants freedom *now,* he cannot understand why the woman on relief does not go out and get a job. He cannot understand why the teenage boy drops out of school. He cannot understand why the high school girl becomes pregnant. His inability or unwillingness to comprehend the plight of others breeds alienation. This person also stands in great need of the reconciling love of God.

To a limited extent this ministry of understanding *can* be supplied by his local church. It can be done much more effectively if the congregation is made up of a variety of people coming from several social classes and representing several points of view. This will enable him to have contact, in a Christian setting, with the people with whom he is working but whom he does not know.

The dilemma which is described in the opening paragraphs of this chapter is primarily a result, not of the use of conflict in the community organization process, but rather of the social, economic, and geographical compartmentalization of urban society. This compartmentalization is reflected in the churches. Thus a typical suburban congregation may be made up exclusively of the "haves" of society while the membership of the inner city church often is drawn largely from the "have nots." This places the burden of reconciling these alienated groups on the church at large. Since the church life of most laymen is centered in their local church, it becomes very difficult to carry on a ministry of reconciliation across congregational boundaries which reflect class lines.

Three answers are often suggested as a solution. The first is the "metropolitan" church which draws people together from all corners of the city. While many local churches do draw from a large geographical area, most of these churches usually continue to be one-class congregations. The so-called "metropolitan" churches usually are representative of the metropolis in geographical terms, not in terms of social class. Rarely are they in a position to fulfill this need for a reconciling ministry across the class lines.

The second approach is the practice mentioned in the beginning of this chapter. Sometimes this involves pairing a well-to-do suburban church with an inner city congregation. Other times it may be based on the establishment of a "sector plan" which includes several different congregations.[5] Either method has severe built-in institutional limitations, and seldom does it result in more than a few people from any one congregation becoming well acquainted with people in other congregations.

The third possibility, and this appears to have the most promise, would be to take advantage of existing denominational relationships and develop a stronger sense of fellowship across congregational lines within one denomination. Perhaps this could be expressed in terms of a goal of having only one Methodist congregation, one United Presbyterian congregation, one Episcopal parish, or one United Church of Christ congregation in each metropolitan area. This "larger parish" could be divided into several subgroups resembling current congregations for certain functions, but the primary organization for fellowship, administration, social action, and corporate worship would be the larger unit.[6] This would provide the structure whereby the urban church could overcome the secular patterns of racial, economic, and social segregation and once again become a sharing and reconciling fellowship.

In addition to this ministry which is aimed at helping the affluent understand the plight of the deprived, the church also

[5] This concept of the sector plan received widespread attention after it had been proposed by Gibson Winter in his book *The Suburban Captivity of the Churches* (Garden City: Doubleday & Co., 1961), pp. 145-71.

[6] For an elaboration of this concept see Lyle E. Schaller, *Planning for Protestantism in Urban America* (Nashville: Abingdon Press, 1965), pp. 161-66.

has a pastoral ministry to the individuals themselves, each of whom has his own set of problems. The importance of this ministry should not be underestimated, but it is a ministry which can be provided within the conventional congregational framework of the local church.

Perhaps the clearest way to summarize this aspect of the churches' participation in the community organization process is to think in terms of primary purposes and responsibilities. The primary purpose of community organization is to help individuals develop and use the resources God has given in controlling their own destiny and the destiny of their communities. This may require accelerating the pace or altering the direction of social change; it may require the use of conflict; it may result in an increase in the degree of alienation. The unique task of the church is to add to this process the dimensions of love, justice, redemption, reconciliation, mercy, and the judgment of God.

Chapter Eight

# Another Point of View

The central question in an evaluation of community organization revolves around a single issue. Is it possible to solve the social and economic problems of contemporary American society through the existing institutionalized structures such as municipal government, the public school system, voluntary health and welfare agencies, labor unions, and business organizations? Or can some of these problems be solved only by the creation of ad hoc agencies which depend upon indigenous leadership and are free to use conflict to achieve social change?

Many of the supporters of the community organization process contend that this is no longer a relevant question. They argue that the existing institutional structures have failed to solve the problems of poverty, race relations, education of the children of the dispossessed, urban blight, and housing. They insist that it is either impossible or too late to reform these structures and that new forms must be found to attack these pressing problems.

Another group of American citizens contends that these problems can best be solved through the efforts of governmental, labor, business, welfare, and other existing agencies. Many of these people argue that the introduction of new ad hoc groups into the decision-making process only complicates the problem and frequently creates unnecessary delays. As an example of this they may cite instances where the net effect of the community organization process has been to completely halt all efforts to eliminate slums and blight by organizing a neighborhood around an anti-urban renewal slogan.

Some insist that the proliferation of civil rights groups, many of which are far more militant than the Urban League and the National Association for the Advancement of Colored People, has hampered the work of these two established organizations, and they add that the use of conflict has alienated so many Caucasians that it is now impossible to expect a solution to the race problem in our generation.

Others will point to the "successes" of community organization as perhaps the most critical element in the current attack on local government in the nation's large cities. They argue, and with the support of a considerable body of historical evidence, that the city government and the public school system have done more for the poor, the members of minority groups, and the slum dwellers than have any of the other structures of our urban society. They will point to the fact that the Negro has found in city hall fewer barriers to employment because of his race than anywhere else he has turned. They can point to the thousands of public housing units built specifically to provide better accommodations for low income families. They will cite the fact that many of the new school buildings and most of the new health clinics in any large city have been constructed in the neighborhoods where live the poor and the dispossessed. They can prove their contention that a disproportionately large share of all local public expenditures is spent to help those people who are now being organized to hate city hall. Finally, they will add that all of this has been accomplished despite the consistent opposition of the wealthy, the real estate interests, and most of the interests representing the "haves."

Officials of local government find themselves baffled by the current anti-city hall attitudes of so many of the proponents of community organization. They ask, "Why are you turning on the people who have been your best friends? Don't you realize that your tactics are playing right into the hands of the Birchers, the real estate lobby, and the other groups who oppose every expansion of public services? What do you want to do, throw out the present responsible political leaders and replace them with a demogogue?"

The author of this book is a firm believer in the value of the community organization process and recognizes that the use of conflict often is essential to the effecting of social change. It is probable that most of the persons who have read this far have an affirmative interest in the subject. Despite this bias on the part of both the writer and the reader, it is possible to recognize that another point of view does exist. It is shared by many thoughtful persons of good will and by many individuals who are in responsible positions of leadership and influence. It is a point of view which should be considered by everyone concerned with community organization.

The major objection raised by those holding this other point of view is that too often efforts at community organization turn out to be destructive attacks on the institutionalized structures of society which have the responsibility, the authority, and the interest in solving the problems that provide the basis for the organization of a new community council.

They argue that while the problems of blight, racial segregation, and housing provide the basic reasons for the creation of a community council, this new organization seldom addresses itself directly to these problems. Instead it focuses its attack on those who have a responsibility for solving the problem.

Thus if the problem is a shortage of decent, safe, and sanitary housing for low income families, the community organization is liable to halt the urban renewal program which will demolish substandard housing and provide sites for the construction of new housing. Or instead of supporting the local housing authority in its running battle with the real estate lobby over the construction of additional units of low rent public housing, the protesters will picket the offices of the manager of the housing authority.

If the problem is one of segregated schools, the leadership of the community council is more likely to engage in a running battle with the board of education or with the superintendent of schools rather than with the white suburbanites who perpetuate the patterns of residential segregation which result in segregated schools.

If the problem is one of inadequate welfare payments for the persons on relief, the community organization process is likely to produce an attack on the local welfare officials or on the city or county governing body, rather than on the political party which controls the state legislature and thereby determines how much money will be available for most categories of public assistance.

These critics of community organization point out that the net result of such tactics is to alienate the natural allies of the poor, the oppressed, and the downtrodden and play right into the hands of those who prefer the minimum level of governmental activity.

This can be seen most clearly in the field of urban renewal

—a program which had bipartisan political support from its beginnings in 1949. Gradually, however, it has been coming under attack from the radical right, but these attacks have had little effect on the pace of the program. More recently, however, urban renewal projects in Boston, Chicago, and dozens of other cities have been brought to a halt—some permanently, some temporarily—by neighborhood associations. Through the use of fear, distrust, and alienation these groups have secured enough power to block renewal plans. However, they have neither the power nor the authority to initiate or implement a proposal of their own. The result is a deadlock, and the two parties with the greatest stake in a successful renewal effort cancel out each other.

This group of critics, who tend to be progovernment in their point of view and favor cooperation over conflict, point to two other areas in which they believe the militant advocates of community organization may be doing more harm than good.

The first is the impact on the efforts to recruit able personnel for positions in local government. The rapid increase in the size and complexity of local government makes it imperative that both appointive and elective positions be filled by persons of ability and character. The mounting attack on city hall makes this increasingly difficult.

When well-trained men with a deep sense of dedication to public service are villified for things they have not done or for conditions over which they have no control, they are tempted to accept the next job offer from a private business which offers them a much higher salary and better working conditions. "I don't mind working for a lower salary, but there is a limit to how much abuse I am willing to take," is the way they justify their vocational switch. They may have weathered several years of attack from the antigovernment and low tax groups without being disturbed. However, when the people they see as their friends and allies, the people whom they have been trying to help, begin to attack them, it hurts. Perhaps the complaints are justified on the grounds of paternalism. Perhaps they grow out of a widening difference in the definition of the public interest. Perhaps they are an inevitable by-product of rapid social change. Regardless of the cause, they have had an adverse effect on the morale of public servants, and some people hold the community organizer responsible for this drop in morale.

The second criticism from this quarter centers on the use of discontent and conflict in the community organization. The contention is made that this inevitably increases the degree of alienation between various segments of the larger community. The result in the words of one observer is to ". . . alienate the neighborhood from the city as a whole rather than bring it into the normal pattern of civic action." [1]

The spirit of cooperation and the search for the common good is replaced by conflict, alienation, polarization, and a struggle for power. Suspicion, fear, and distrust cloud the atmosphere and inhibit the discussions and meeting which are called to work out agreement on a common course of action but usually end in a stalemate. The time and energy which might have been devoted to developing new approaches to complex problems are spent in identifying and villifying the "enemy" or in working out counter moves to thwart the next attack.

What started out to be a creative expression of citizen participation in community decision-making turns into a process which divides the community into several hostile camps. As the degree of alienation grows, it becomes increasingly difficult to make

[1] Wilson, "Planning and Politics," p. 246.

decisions on a rational basis and the whole decision-making process is turned upside down.

The impact that alienation can have on the decision-making process is illustrated by a referendum on a tax levy for schools held in Cleveland in May, 1964. During the previous decade the public had been very reluctant to vote additional taxes for the Cleveland school system, and the normal election found a majority of whites voting against the levy with a majority of Negroes voting in favor of the school tax. Because the Negro voters were a minority, it usually required an overwhelmingly favorable vote in the Negro wards for a school issue to be approved.

The 1963-64 school year witnessed a major protest by the Negro community against the schools of Cleveland. The protests resulted in the elimination of the half-day classes for Negro pupils, a minor reduction in school segregation, and other improvements. The board of education also finally faced up to the need for additional taxes but was not very optimistic about getting the necessary voter support since most of the extra funds would be spent in the Negro wards and the white voters, over one half of whom did not have any children in the public schools, obviously would be reluctant to vote for the levy.

By the time the May referendum came around the degree of alienation between the board of education, and especially with the board president, who appeared to be the major enemy of the civil rights movement, and the Negro community had reached its peak. In this situation many of the leaders of the Negro protest either opposed or took no position on the tax levy which the board president strongly supported. By election day the tax levy, which really was a measure for financing the operation of the public schools, was interpreted by many as a confidence vote in the board president who symbolized the resistance to the civil rights movement. The tax levy carried overwhelmingly in the white wards which normally opposed taxes for the schools! It lost in several Negro wards which stood to benefit the most from the levy!

When community organization causes this kind of breakdown in the normal and predictable decision-making process, say these critics, the entire structure of government is threatened.

Perhaps the most disturbing criticism of the community organization process is offered by those who contend that the neighborhood unit does not have the importance nor the values attributed to it for the past forty years. The persons holding this point of view assert that the geographical neighborhood is not a natural unit for interpersonal relationships in an urban society and that the neighborhood unit in fact acts as a device for maintaining racial, ethnic, cultural, economic, and social segregation.

This sounds like heresy to most community planners who have been basing their planning concepts on the neighborhood unit ever since Clarence Perry initiated the idea in his report to the New York Regional Plan Association in 1926. It has the sound of heresy to most pastors and denominational executives who have been operating on the premise that the local church should serve the residents of its neighborhood. It is a threatening criticism to the church planners who have based their plans for new church development, their program proposals for established churches, and their pleas for interdenominational cooperation on an acceptance of the neighborhood unit.[2]

[2] For a more detailed statement of this point of view see Reginald R. Isaacs, "Are Urban Neighborhoods Possible?" *Journal of Housing*, V (July, 1948), 177-80; Isaacs, "The Neighborhood Unit," *Journal of Housing* (August, 1948), 215-19; Ellen Lurie, "Is There a Conflict?" *The City Church*, November-Decem-

This criticism is most disturbing to the advocates of community organization who have accepted the idea that the neighborhood is the unit in which a person desires to live and to maintain his primary face-to-face contacts. It is assumed that a "good" neighborhood is one in which there is a low degree of mobility among the residents and a "poor" neighborhood is one with a high transiency rate. It is assumed that a desirable social goal is the reduction of transiency and the promotion of long tenure among the residents. It is assumed that the institutions in the neighborhood should serve the nearby residents and that the residents should patronize the neighborhood institutions. It is assumed that the individual can experience the greatest personal growth if he feels himself to be a part of a community *which can be identified in geographical terms*. It is assumed that anyone who works to promote stability in a neighborhood is on the side of the angels and those who favor change are agents of the devil. It is assumed that the geographical neighborhood is the logical basic unit for organizing political action efforts, for meeting the educational needs of children, and for providing a religious ministry to people.

All these assumptions have been incorporated into the basic foundations of community organization. All these assumptions are now being challenged.

The first major rejection of these assumptions came from the Protestant churches which long ago abandoned the concept of a geographical parish in favor of a nongeographical parish which was determined by such characteristics as language, national origin, place of birth, race, age, income, social status, place where one first joined the church, occupation, sentiment, and

ber, 1964, pp. 5-9; Glenn H. Beyer, *Housing and Society* (New York: The Macmillan Company, 1965), pp. 317-18.

theological beliefs. It is important to note that this rejection of the neighborhood concept came from the local church as an institution, only occasionally from the pastor, and rarely from the denominational executive.

Later the neighborhood concept was rejected by state boards of education which first encouraged, and subsequently forced, the elimination of the neighborhood school in rural areas. Eventually these state educational agencies encouraged the elimination of neighborhood schools in many urban areas through large subsidies for bus transportation programs and extra financial assistance for the larger school.

As Negroes moved into the urban north, they, too, rejected the neighborhood concept in favor of continued loyalty to the larger Negro community. Thus the first Negroes to move into a previously all-white neighborhood seldom attempted to patronize the neighborhood church, doctor, dentist, barber, or druggist. Instead they continued to maintain their ties with the Negro church, doctor, dentist, barber, or druggist who was a part of the nongeographical Negro community. (It is true that many Negroes in these circumstances maintained their ties with the Negro community because they were not free to establish new relationships in their geographical neighborhood. This has been a factor, but it is not the only consideration in this decision. The same pattern can be observed among Caucasians who move to a new neighborhood and who do not face the color barrier.)

More recently some of these assumptions are being challenged in the prestige suburban neighborhoods which are not subject to racial tensions. In these "good" neighborhoods there is a high rate of mobility as young executives buy homes, move in, and a year later find themselves offered better jobs in another city. In these "good" neighborhoods the residents attend a great variety of churches, most of which are located outside that community. The residents drive five or ten miles to a regional shopping center to shop, their children are transported by bus to a school four miles from their home, and the bulk of the interpersonal relationships of the adults are with persons who live in other neighborhoods. Nearly every adult male leaves the neighborhood when he goes to work, and many are away from home from Monday morning until Friday evening.

In these circumstances what is the community in which a community organization process is to be developed?

These criticisms are strengthened by the fact that all too often the argument for "stability" was really an attempt to keep Negroes out; the plea for residents to patronize the neighborhood church, the corner grocery, or the local YMCA was made with the hidden hope that this would increase the vigor and health of these institutions and businesses; and the drive for a local clean-up campaign was supported by many who saw the possibility of economic benefits for themselves.

Both of these other points of view deserve the attention of the churchman interested in community organization. The first is the perspective of the person who is actively involved in the established structures of society. Naturally such a person will tend to view with grave reservations any process or movement which may threaten the stability or influence of the social structure of which he is a part.

The second point of view is shared by many persons who do not have a vested interest in the status quo, but rather are seeking a clearer understanding of reality.

Three other points of view merit at least brief mention here, for each represents a group of persons who are skeptical of the whole concept of community organization as it has been practiced in America.

The first of these is shared by many Negroes who point out that thus far the greatest participation by churches in community organizations of one form or another has been in those communities which felt threatened by the probable influx of Negroes. There are many exceptions to this pattern, but the greatest single stimulus to participation by the local church has been the fear of Negroes. It is true that some of these neighborhood associations which were organized to perpetuate residential segregation eventually substituted more constructive goals. However, many did not. For example, Saul Alinsky's first famous effort at community organization in Chicago turned out to be an effort to keep Negroes out of the Back of the Yards district of that city.

Inasmuch as many of the recent efforts at community organization in which the churches have been notably active do include neighborhoods with a large Negro population, this point of view deserves serious consideration.

Serious criticism of the community organization process is offered by a group of persons holding a quite different point of view. These critics contend that the community organization process is too slow and unwieldy. They contend that the pace of change in modern society is so fast that the rest of the larger community cannot wait for a smaller group to organize and respond to the changing conditions.

This group includes several historians who tend to a larger view of the world. It includes many of the more militant civil rights leaders who contend that in view of world conditions and the image of America abroad, the desegregation process cannot wait for the Negro to get organized to promote racial equality, nor can it wait for the community organization process to change the attitudes of whites who are reluctant to accept the elimination of racial barriers. They point to the fair employment practices laws enacted in northern states in the 1940's and 1950's as the model for imposing social change on the masses.

The basic position of this group is that in modern American society a democratic elite can move faster, more responsibly, and more creatively in responding to the challenges of a complex world than can a cumbersome citizens association. Furthermore, they argue, when this planning by a democratic elite is carried on under governmental auspices it is perfectly compatible with the American political system and the concept of representative government.

These critics also suggest that the necessity of rebuilding our cities is so urgent that the nation cannot afford the luxury of citizen participation in the renewal effort. The task is so large, the decisions are so complex, and the need so great that there is not enough time left to develop and implement a program designed to give the poor and the powerless an opportunity to participate in the planning.

In support of their position this group can point to the Economic Opportunity Act of 1964—a program designed to assist those living in poverty—which was developed by a democratic elite with practically no help from the poor and only limited assistance from persons in daily contact with the poor. They insist that this procedure produced a good bill in a very short period of time which was acceptable to the Congress and to the country at large and which offered a realistic beginning program for the war on poverty.

These same supporters of decision-making by a democratic elite find additional support for their position in the contrasting systems of local taxation in the United States. In some states the general property tax rate for local govermental purposes is set by the elected representatives of the people—a democratic elite. The city council or the board of education can set the rate as high as it feels is necessary to finance the necessary level of public services. The voters have no recourse except to "turn the rascals out" at the next election.

In other states there is a ceiling, usually a very low ceiling, on the rate the elected officials can levy without going to the voters in a referendum. Thus the people have a veto power over every proposed increase in the general property tax rate.

Many observers contend that where the decision on the tax rate is left solely in the hands of the elected officials the level of public services is superior to those states where each increase in the tax rate has to be submitted to the electorate. If one accepts the premise that the purpose of government is to provide services to the public, this can be interpreted as an argument on behalf of the democratic elite theory.

At the opposite end of the philosophical spectrum are those critics of community organization who insist that the community organization process is an artificial effort which unduly interferes with the way people want to live. If a person is content to live in poverty, he should be allowed to do so. If he does not want to be a part of the community decision-making process, he has a right to stay home. No one, including the well-intended community organizer or a member of the power elite, has either the right or the ability to play God and manipulate the lives of the poor and the powerless. While the supporters of this position appear to be the least numerous of the five groups presented in this chapter, they do represent a significant point of view.

Chapter Nine

# Lessons from Experience

It was the third meeting of the newly formed Glenwood Community Association which had been organized by the metropolitan welfare council. The association had been organized to help the people in Glenwood identify and solve some of the problems which plagued the neighborhood. The pastor of St. Luke's Lutheran Church had helped to initiate this experience in community organization and the association met monthly in the basement of his church. On this particular evening there were nineteen persons present—four men and fifteen women—when the chairman called the meeting to order. After the minutes of the last meeting had been read, a woman in her forties rose and was recognized.

"I came here tonight," she stated in a tone of indignation, "to see what this group can do about a real problem we have. Just three blocks from here is Frank's Tavern, and for the past two weeks the bartender has been attempting to entice our teenage girls to go into the tavern. What can this group do to put a stop to this?"

The chairman turned to the staff worker from the welfare council who had been assigned to help organize the community association. He stood up and faced the woman who had voiced the complaint. "You have raised a most important issue, and it deserves immediate attention. Tomorrow morning I'll take this matter to the inter-agency committee. They are really powerful people and should be able to handle this problem with no difficulty."

The rest of the evening was devoted largely to a discussion of how attendance could be increased and of various ways to get more men to attend. Just before adjournment a committee was appointed to provide cookies and punch at the next meeting.

In commenting on this incident, Stanley Hallett, who has been actively involved in community organization in Chicago, suggested that the chairman or staff adviser might have said, "Next Thursday evening tell all your husbands to be sure to be here at seven o'clock. We'll go down to the tavern and tell the bartender this has to stop now!"

If this had been done it would have (1) solved the problem of the bartender luring young girls into the tavern, (2) provided the opportunity for the residents to gain a sense of their own power—instead the staff adviser inferred they had no power and the "really powerful people" were outsiders, and (3) produced a far larger attendance at the next meeting than could be achieved by serving cookies and punch.

## The Use of Discontent

This episode illustrates two of the basic lessons in community organization which have been tested and proved by experience. The first of these is the usefulness of discontent. Discontent is the prime motivation for action in community organization. The indignant woman voiced discontent with the tactics of the bartender. She had a legitimate complaint, and it could have been used as a rallying point for putting some life and meaning into what was obviously a lethargic organization. Murray Ross has commented that to be effective discontent must be channeled into the problem-solving process in respect to specific problems.[1] In addition the discontent must be widely shared if it is to be an important stimulant to organization. In this case both conditions prevailed, but no one recognized a valuable issue when it was handed to them.

## The Value of Direct Action

The second lesson illustrated by Hallett's comment on this episode is the value of direct action. On many occasions a direct approach is the quickest and most effective method for solving simple problems. If the husbands and fathers of Glenwood had gathered and marched as a group to Frank's Tavern, they probably would have persuaded the bartender that he should mend his ways. The decision made by the staff person to carry this problem to a committee of the welfare council guaranteed delay and was far less certain to produce a solution.

Direct action also helps weld a heterogenous group of people together into a unified organization. Here again the adviser to the group failed to grasp an opportunity. If fifteen to twenty men had marched together down to Frank's Tavern, they would have remembered the occasion for years afterward and associated that experience with the Glenwood Community Association. This would have given each man, and his wife, a sense of being an important member of a lively and dynamic organization.

[1] *Community Organization*, pp. 156-64.

155

## Interfaith Cooperation

The experience of the Christian churches in community organization also has produced a variety of other lessons on the subject. Perhaps none is more timely than the lesson in interfaith cooperation. While it is impossible to measure such a subjective issue, it appears that seldom if ever before has there been the degree of interfaith cooperation on the American religious scene as has been engendered by recent efforts in achieving social change. One area of cooperation has been in the civil rights movement with the organization of scores of national, state, and local interfaith agencies on religion and race. Earlier there were dozens of meaningful interfaith experiences as Protestants and Roman Catholics worked together through the community organization process to provide a ministry for migrant farm laborers. More recently similarly interfaith groups have been formed to join in the war on poverty. In Chicago, Detroit, Rochester, Kansas City, and other urban centers Roman Catholic and Protestant churches have joined together in community organization efforts. In these ventures the degree of cooperation has been far greater and much more active than in either the race relations or antipoverty fields.

Out of these varied experiences it has become increasingly apparent that interfaith cooperation can work. The central lesson to be gained from these experiences, and one which perhaps can be seen most clearly in the community organization process, is that when the religious leaders of various faiths come together in these circumstances they do not come to talk about their theological differences. Rather they come together to identify the problems which beset a community and to explore ways to solve these problems. The family of man under God finds itself with a common vision which more than offsets the theological differences which have divided that family. While it is not necessary for the establishment of a viable interfaith relationship, it appears that the use of conflict as a means of achieving social change does act as a kind of cement which helps to strengthen the ties across faith lines. It should not be inferred from this, however, that the use of conflict is the key to effective interfaith cooperation. That key is the combination of social action and sense of mission which is essential to a church's effective participation in any movement to achieve social change.

## The Evangelical Dimension

A strong argument can be made that every program, every activity, every emphasis, every element of the church's ministry cannot be justified unless it has a clearcut evangelical dimension. Support for this argument can be mustered from the Scriptures. Support can be found in the sterile results of many church programs ranging from bowling leagues in the local church to denominationally supported housing projects for the elderly and from the men's club which meets to hear a public relations speech by the high school football coach to church-supported hospitals. Support for this argument can be found in the statistical records of too many local churches which carry on a "ministry" to the community, but never win any converts from outside the church family.

Is the process of community organization a function which the church as an evangelical religious institution and the Christian as an evangelistically minded individual can participate in, or is it a diversion from their evangelistic responsibilities? The experiences of hundreds of churches and scores of community organization and community development programs overwhelmingly supports the contention that these efforts are compatible with and supportive of the local church's role as an evangelist.

There are at least three facets to this question. Most obvious is the fact that the community organization process has helped individuals develop the courage and skill to participate in the life of their own community. This has meant that many persons have been encouraged to come out of their shell and to accept leadership responsibilities. They begin to feel important, to feel that they are wanted, to feel they have a contribution to offer. As this happens they are freed to move out of the back pews and into the active life of the congregation. Others, who were not participating in the life of any local church, are freed to come into what previously had appeared to be a closed community. As these new community leaders emerge from nowhere, the local churches, always short on leadership, usually are quick to recognize this new resource and to seek a new relationship to the individual. (Whether the local church does this out of a sense of evangelism or merely to exploit the ability of a new community leader is another question.)

Second, and far more important, is the fact that the participation by the local church and its members is a witness to their Christian concern and an expression of their convictions. It means the church moves out to "where the action is," where man is living his daily life in the world. When people outside the church see Christians offering this kind of witness, the church cannot help being impressive and attract those who wonder why people would do this. In the Gospel According to Matthew we are advised to let our light shine forth so men may see and give glory to our Father in heaven. The community organization process is one way of responding to that imperative.

The third lesson that experience has taught is that the evangelistic dimension should not be given primary emphasis, but rather regarded as a fringe benefit. In other words, it is better to place the primary emphasis on the human resource development and the service aspects of community organization and let this witness to the power of the gospel be the message to those outside the church. Any other course entails the risk that the people may feel, and perhaps with good reason, that the church is seeking to exploit them for the glory of the local church. The distinctive form of the New Testament church is servanthood. The community organization process is highly compatible with that form, and the church can be a most persuasive evangelist when it is fulfilling its function as servant.

## Social Action Dimension

Churches which have been actively involved in the community organization process frequently report that this has provided the members with their first opportunity to express their Christian convictions *through the church*. Too often laymen feel that the church is too ingrown, too conservative, and too institutionalized. They find themselves repeatedly frustrated as they seek to respond *through the church* to the imperative of the gospel which is preached in the church.

By involving itself in the community organization process the church can offer its members a thrilling opportunity to actively apply their beliefs to the process of planned social change. Lest anyone be misled into thinking this is an automatic reaction, it should be noted here that in a larger number of congregations this type of participation would be considered too threatening to the institutional stability of the church for it to receive official encouragement from the governing board of the congregation. For those churches and churchmen who are sufficiently secure to participate, the community organization process can add a new dimension to the life of the congregation as it hears the gospel and then is given this added opportunity to respond.

There is a variety of ways the church can participate in community organization, and many of these may closely resemble the participation of secular institutions. Experience suggests three roles that are especially appropriate for the churches.

The first of these is the church's role as an identifier of the problems of the community. The pastor and the members of the local church should be in an excellent position to recognize the problems which adversely affect their community. Furthermore, the church, its pastor, and its members should be free to do this. The church should be free of the vested interests and the repressive forces which seek to conceal or disguise these problems. Whether it be inadequate enforcement of the housing code, abuses by the liquor industry, corruption in public office, dishonest merchants, racial prejudice, or inferior schools, the church should be able and willing to identify these problems and assist in the formulation of community goals.

A second role for the church is that of a prophet. The church should reserve for itself the right to evaluate the goals of the community council, to criticize both ends and means, and to bring the light of the Christian ethic to bear on the problem-solving process.

Finally, the church may at times be the only institution in the community with both the freedom and the financial resources necessary to provide the community with an able change agent. This change agent may be charged with the responsibility for identifying the problems which other interests are trying to sweep under the rug. He may be an enabler or organizer. He may serve as an advocate for the residents as they attempt to fight their own battles for justice and equality. Whatever the exact nature of his role, it is becoming increasingly apparent that in some communities only the church is able to provide the neighborhood with the assistance of a full-time professional change agent.

## The Problems of Finances

Perhaps the clearest lessons to come out of recent experience have been related to money. How can this effort be financed? How much money is necessary? Is it possible to use "outside" sources of funds without jeopardizing the entire effort?

Experience indicates that an effective community organization can be built only on a sound financial base. This is especially true in low income areas where the recruitment and training of indigenous leaders is a slow and expensive process. The record of Saul Alinsky and the Industrial Areas Foundation suggests that this lesson has been learned well. Alinsky will not undertake an organizing effort unless adequate financing has been guaranteed. This may be $50,000 a year or more. For example, during the 1950's the Back of the Yards Council in Chicago had a total budget averaging around $75,000 a year.

Several specialists in the field contend that as a rule-of-thumb it costs one dollar per year per resident to organize a community and that much more to maintain a vital organization. Others contend that this figure it too low. Regardless of the exact amount of money required, it is now very apparent that the effectiveness of any community organization effort is directly related to the amount of money available to it.

Very closely related to this need for rather large sums of money is the obvious requirement that there be no strings attached to the money. The experience in Cleveland and elsewhere with community councils which are financed through the local united appeal has demonstrated the vulnerability of these organizations to pressures from those who seek to preserve the status quo. The independence of any voluntary organization is jeopardized when it is dependent on contributions which may be given with reservations or completely withheld.

The importance of this lesson is so great that three methods have been proposed to reduce or eliminate the problem. One of these has been for the churches to provide large financial grants for local efforts in community organization. If these grants come through denominational channels it greatly reduces the possibility that the initial donor will be able to attach any restrictions to his gift. The denominational agencies, as the immediate grantors, have not seen fit to use their financial power as a club over the local program.

A second proposed solution has been to establish a local or metropolitan nonprofit corporation which could receive funds from individuals, corporations, and foundations and then allocate these to specific community organization activities. This would provide an intermediary agency between the donor and the eventual recipient and thus eliminate or reduce the restrictions which might accompany the gift and the repercussions which could adversely affect the donor. This approach has three drawbacks. First of all, there is a major legal question over the tax exemption of gifts to such an intermediary foundation. Presumably it would be vulnerable to the charge that its grants were going to organizations engaged in political activities since much of the current activity of contemporary community councils is in the political arena. Second, the idea is predicated on the assumption that this new foundation would receive gifts directly from other philanthropic foundations. This is questionable, since most foundations operate on the principle that they are responsible for the use of the funds entrusted to them and they cannot delegate this trust to another party. Third, all donors always have the right to withhold further gifts and the intermediary foundation would be vulnerable to this fact of life.

The third proposal to solve the financial problem is the oldest. This is to raise the funds from the residents and institutions within the community itself, thus eliminating the issue of "outside control." The limitations of this idea are self-evident in a low income neighborhood where *anomie* is a dominant characteristic of the people. It is for this reason that churches and foundations are being asked for money.

The one lesson is clear, community organization requires rather large sums of money; but the related lesson on how this money can be raised is still being learned.

## The Lesson on Conflict

The experience of the community organization process has paralleled the pattern of social movements in several ways, but one of these parallels stands out above all others and merits the thoughtful consideration of every churchman interested in this subject. This is the tendency to move from a basic reliance on the use of conflict toward increased use of cooperation.

The pattern is very clear and repeated frequently. An ad hoc group is organized and functions around the theme of conflict. As time passes it begins to acquire recognition, legitimacy, and acceptance. When this occurs it begins to move away from the use of conflict and to place a greater emphasis on negotiation and cooperation with the established structures and institutions of society.

It would be only a slight exaggeration to summarize this trend by saying that conflict may be a useful technique to gain a seat at the bargaining table, but the bargaining conducted by those seated at this table tends to emphasize compromise and cooperation.

Finally, it should be noted that most persons who have closely observed or actively participated in the community organization process tend to agree on one very basic lesson. Community organization cannot and will not solve all of the social, economic, and political ills of society, but it is a very significant method for helping people help themselves—and this may be the way the Christian churches can be most effective in helping to solve many of the problems of the world.

# Questions for Christians

The purpose of this book has not been to present the reader with a series of answers to all his questions about community organization. Rather, the purpose has been to provide an introduction to the community organization process, a brief description of how it reached its present state, and a basic foundation for consideration of the fundamental questions which should be answered by the churchman who is interested in this process of providing new opportunities for human resource development and of effecting social change.

Several of these questions have been discussed in some detail in earlier chapters, others were mentioned only in passing, and a few appear here for the first time. The purpose of these pages is to present these questions in a manner which will be helpful to the individual or to a group of churchmen in evaluating the community organization process. It is based on the assumption that the first step in a systematic approach to any problem is to ask the right questions. It is hoped that this chapter will help the Christian who has an interest in community organization ask the right questions.

1. Does the present state of American society require the creation of ad hoc organizations to solve specific questions? Does the future of American democracy depend on the development of new organizational forms which encourage more widespread participation in the community decision-making process?

2. Can a community organization be expected to be more than another group with the power to veto, but without enough power to initiate or implement? Is there a danger that a community council may tackle problems far beyond the technical competence of its members and thus end up being only a needless roadblock in the path of progress?

3. Does the community organization process really help people grow and realize their own potential? Has the idea of recruiting and training indigenous leadership been overly romanticized?

4. If a church participates in a community organization venture on the basis that this is human resource development and that this will help the oppressed realize a sense of selfhood, what happens when the self that is manifested does not coincide with the dreams of the churchmen who sponsored the venture? Will the church be thrilled that a sense of self has emerged or feel threatened because it emerges in a different form than was anticipated?

5. Today the church is being called on to help finance new ventures in community organization. What happens when the self-determined goals of a community conflict with the values of the church which financed the beginnings of the venture? What should the church expect of a community organization which it helps start but expects to be self-determining?

6. Which is the appropriate *primary* motivation for the church's involvement in the community organization process, human re-

source development, influencing the course of planned social change, or the redistribution of power? Does this raise any problems if other participants in the same venture have different primary motives?

7. Is it appropriate for the local church as an institution to become a member of a community council? Or should the church remain outside the council but encourage its members to become active participants? Or should the church not take any official position on this matter of membership and participation?

8. Is the acquisition of power necessary to influence the course of social change?

9. Does the church tend to expect the people to organize and to use power in a manner that seems right to the church or in a manner that seems right to the people themselves?

10. Do the poor and the dispossessed have to feel a sense of power before they can be expected to take the initiative in defining and solving their own problems? If this is true, is it morally right to create an artificial issue which will enable them to feel a sense of power?

11. Does the creation of a community council automatically endow it with a quantity of power greater than the sum of the power held by the member organizations before they came together? If so, who loses the power gained by the formation of the community council? Or is it true that someone can gain power without anyone else necessarily losing some power? Is power a fixed quantity, or can it be enlarged?

12. Does a community or a group have to possess some degree of power to be truly *free* participants in the decision-making process?

13. In American society do the "rights" of some people inevitably result in a denial or oppression of the "rights" of other people?

14. The community organization process is based on a belief in the right of self-determination. How far can the "outsider" go in helping indigenous leaders acquire power? What is the appropriate response for the outside adviser when these indigenous leaders select what he considers to be morally wrong goals? What is the natural response of this outsider when the indigenous leadership subsequently decides it can dispense with his help? Is there a parallel in the foreign mission field?

15. Is conflict necessary to effect social change? If it is, how can the alienation which accompanies conflict be kept from becoming a permanent polarization? If it is necessary to "rub raw the sores of discontent," how does one know when he has rubbed enough?

16. Is there a tendency for organizations, which are organized on the premise that conflict is the fastest method of achieving social change, to move away from the use of conflict and toward greater use of cooperation? If the use of conflict is accepted as a proper means for organizing a community, how can one later "demobilize" those participants who may have come to enjoy the excitement of conflict and prefer this to the less dramatic patterns of cooperation and collaboration? Is there a danger that the use of conflict will divide the protesters into two groups, (a) those who primarily are interested in achieving social change, and (b) those who are primarily interested in the excitement and thrill of conflict?

17. Can conflict and the threat of conflict bring the "haves" to a compassionate understanding of the plight of the oppressed, or does it widen the gap between the "haves" and the "have nots"?

18. Can there be conflict within an atmosphere of love? Are justice and love incompatible motivations or goals in community organization?

19. Which is the more appropriate method for the Christian to stress as he seeks to influence the course of social change, cooperation or conflict? Which is the more effective?

20. Can the Christian be opposed to the means used to achieve a desirable end when he knows that his opposition to the means guarantees the end will never be accomplished? Does this make him an opponent of both the means and the end?

21. Is it reasonable to expect an existing institution to support a community organization effort which may threaten that institution? Is it realistic to expect local governments to encourage the organization of the poor under Title II of the Economic Opportunity Act of 1964 when it is inevitable that this will threaten existing power centers and political alliances? Is it realistic to expect a church which does not serve the residents of the neighborhood in which the building is located to support, and perhaps join, a community council in that neighborhood?

22. Frequently the church is filled with the people who have fled from an encounter with the world where conflict and the struggle for power is always occurring. Does this mean that the church in these circumstances is immobilized? Does this force the churchmen who want to engage in this encounter to leave the church and go to a secular organization in order to have a chance to witness to their Christian convictions?

23. Is it possible for the church to use methods about which it has some reservations in organizing a community without ever buying the philosophy or outlook on which these methods are based? Can a community council "use" an outside organizer to carry on the first phase of organizing and then disown him and his methods?

24. If the church seeks to identify with and to help the oppressed, the dispossessed, the disfranchised, and the poor, does this cut the church off from a pastoral responsibility to the rich,

the powerful, and the comfortable? The holders of power may feel threatened by the emergence of a new power bloc. If the church assists in the formation of this new power center, will this alienate the traditional holders of power from the church?

25. Is community organization becoming the new "legitimate" protest party replacing the left wing political parties which have faded from the American political scene? Does the church involvement mean the churches are about to become an active part of the process of launching a new political movement?

Questions such as these merit the serious consideration of every Christian who is seriously interested in the community organization process. The answers he gives to these questions will determine the extent, the nature, and the effectiveness of his participation in this effort to influence the course and pace of social change.

# Index